Cold Hands, Warm Heart

A Memoir

By Grace & Liz Nicholas

Cold Hands, Warm Heart

A Memoir

By Grace & Liz Nicholas

Published by:
Arc Publishing and Print
166 Knowle Lane
Sheffield
S11 9SJ

Telephone: 07809 172872

Email: chris@arcbooks.co.uk

All proceeds from this book will be given to SYEDA
(South Yorkshire Eating Disorders Association)

Contents

Foreword

"Just eat" was said by a loving, sympathetic and caring friend to my daughter when she was in the middle of her eating disorder. However, as can be seen in Grace's story, such simple words cannot be so easily acted upon by someone suffering from anorexia nervosa, yet they are the words which Liz, Ed and all of Grace's family and friends wanted to say.

'Cold Hands, Warm Heart' expresses the fears, difficulties, horrors and confusion experienced by all who are affected by an eating disorder, yet though the journey is difficult at times and there is a feeling of being caught up in a downward spiral, there is hope, there is light at the end of a seemingly endless dark tunnel.

There were so many aspects of Grace's and Liz's story which resonate not only with myself but will with many other sufferers and carers. For example, the lack of urgency and understanding by so many health professionals; of feeling helpless; of not knowing where to get information and help. Grace's experience was one of initially slow onset but once anorexia had taken hold it rapidly spiralled out of control, putting her life in danger.

SYEDA is grateful for Grace and Liz telling their stories because it highlights the need for urgent action; the sooner an eating disorder, particularly anorexia, is treated, before it becomes too entrenched in the mind, the quicker and more long lasting recovery will be. Only the person who is ill can decide to get better which makes it harder for those around the sufferer to help and support them. However, once they have decided to get better, they cannot do so alone, as Grace has shown, they need the love and moreover the support of those around them. Therefore the carers themselves require support, care and education about the illness to enable them to encourage the sufferer towards their recovery and to maintain it, especially once the 'epiphany moment' of wanting to banish the eating disorder occurs. Moreover their story demonstrates that recovery can be achieved, together with the development of improved self-esteem and confidence with one's own body.

Every journey is an individual one. At SYEDA we aim to give encouragement and support to **all** who are affected by an eating disorder and to offer a wide range of services which will give them the motivation, power and resilience in their journey to recovery, to achieve health and well-being.

JENNY ALLEN – Chair SYEDA

(Parent of a daughter who tragically lost her life as a result of anorexia nervosa.)

Introduction

Grace

Anorexia makes you feel alone and afraid. It makes women, men, mothers and fathers, sisters, brothers and friends feel completely alone and that no one understands. That is why it's so important to me that people read this now. I hope it makes people feel understood, knowing there are people who have lived through it, and will continue to live through it. I'm not leading a 'new' life now; I'm still growing from the person I was before, during and after anorexia.

Everyone's experience of this illness is different. This can be a very frustrating thing to hear when all you want is an answer to why someone you know and love has stopped trusting food. Just know that you're never alone. To cut you off from everyone, that's what anorexia wants. For every bad feeling you have about yourself, there are a billion bad feelings about anorexia. It's immeasurably hard to fight something that takes physical form in either your reflection or someone that you love. Just keep loving, don't forget the person you're fighting for. They are still there.

Introduction Liz

This is the story of a strange time. It was intense and difficult, and we have all come out of it slightly different people. I still don't know quite why Grace got ill, and I don't know quite why she got better. But she did, and I value so much every day that we have. Every time I hear her sing or laugh delights me. When I feel her slipping into sadness I have to beat down the panic that she will not come back out of it.

This is just the story of how it felt – to Grace, and to me. We lived the same story but we were in different places. If anyone who reads this has visited those dark places, I hope it makes you feel less lonely. People do come out the other side of anorexia. But it is not a straightforward illness; it can recur after subsiding for years. A recovering alcoholic can actively say no to alcohol; a recovering anorexic cannot avoid the daily choice of eating or not. No one can totally avoid those times where some goblin in our brain whispers, *"I told you you were useless. It's all no good…"* At the moment in our case the demons of anorexia and depression are quiet. Dormant, not extinct.

The beginning

Grace

Results Day 2007 – Late August

Our GCSE results had come out that day. We were all at Sophie's, celebrating in her garden, and my friend Lauren left, to go to the gym. I remember being jealous of her, wishing I was good enough to join a gym – but I didn't dwell on it then. I just enjoyed the day. *"Yeah, maybe I could be a bit healthier but I'm having fun with my friends!"*.

That night we were talking about how much we'd been partying, and Lauren clearly felt guilty, which I thought was very odd. Why feel bad about having a good time? She said she'd only eat rice and steamed veg. for the next week. Instead of thinking a) how dull, why not have some nice food? Or b) that's not a good way to be thinking, should I be worried about my friend? I thought *"Wow, she's got it right – she's clever and gorgeous, maybe I should try that, and I might be happier"*.

But I wasn't sad, or unhealthy, or fat. I was excited for a new start at sixth form, a break from Deirdre (my "best friend" of five years, who had spent most of that time bullying me), and a chance to get to know my other friends better. I'd felt very dependent on Deirdre as she was my closest friend when we moved up to secondary school, I felt like I needed her permission to do pretty much anything involving other friends or boys. She knew this and she used me; when she didn't need me she would forget I existed for a couple of weeks and I'd feel I'd done something wrong. This really messed with my confidence and however much she did it, I'd always go running back to her, desperate for her attention and time. However that summer, after our girly group holiday to Newquay, I started to break away from her. I started being able to talk about how she hurt me to my boyfriend and family and other friends, and they helped me realise she wasn't worth it. She was going to a different 6th form to me and I was feeling bright about my future without her.

Soon after that, I joined the local gym. When I was being shown round I was especially interested in the super-calorie-burning machines.

At first I felt empowered and confident, proud that I was going to the gym, looking after my body. My sister Emily was against it from the start. *"Wouldn't you rather have the money?"* she said. *"You don't need to go, you're perfect ... don't go all stupid and anorexic on me!"*. Obviously I talked my way out of all these reasons not to go, and just made more of an effort to. To make it clear to everyone, myself included, that I was in control.

At school I started my A levels. I was taking Spanish, Politics, Theatre Studies and Art. I was in Mr W's class – he was my drama teacher – with all my closest friends, all over-achievers in almost everything they did. I felt completely inadequate to them; I'd constantly be comparing myself to them – looks, hair, body shape, lifestyle, work, taste in clothes, everything. I didn't really try not to compare myself, because I felt so lucky to have such a great group of people around me. I felt like I should try and change myself to fit in better with them, rather than question it. It's also very normal for teenage girls to discuss each others' merits and faults, it's often how they bond. Either complimenting each other's good points or venting about someone's annoying habits is the basis of many a friendship.

My friendship with Rachel and Rowena in particular was growing and I loved spending time with them. They seemed to really appreciate and like me, which I hadn't had much of from Deirdre. We had a mutual love for musicals and fashion, and very similar senses of humour. I spent more time with people from other friendship groups who I'd not really spoken to before, and it was a nice break from the work-driven friends in my form.

A new girl came to our school and we hung out with her. She made it very clear how she felt about food. *"I don't see how you can all eat lunch together. I don't eat during the day. I think it's disgusting."* Yes, it was irritating, far-fetched, unrealistic and very worrying – but part of me was still jealous of her – she wasn't dependent on food, I thought.

Me and my boyfriend Dan were happy enough. He'd left school after his A-levels the year before and was having a gap year and had a job in a café. We'd been together for over a year and he was my best friend. We weren't seeing each other much because I was so busy; with school, volunteering at a special school, looking after Tilly (my youngest sister), making dinner. Dad was working 5pm-9pm so after school and evenings were always a bit hectic and we stopped having sat down family meals regularly. I also had a Saturday job at the bead shop my older brother Seth worked at.

I started restricting my food in about October/late September. I remember going to a friend's birthday meal, and not having enough money for a proper meal, so I just got garlic bread and said to myself I'd eat when I got back. But for some reason I didn't and felt a strange sense of pride. But it was guilty pride because I knew I didn't want to tell my Mum. At breakfast time I'd started taking my cereal into my room and just drinking the milk. I'd hide the cereal in my bin. It felt a bit like a game. This habit was completely alien though, I'd never purposefully skipped a meal in my life – I knew it was pointless and unhealthy and I loved food. I enjoyed cooking and talking about it with other people, so the way I was behaving didn't compute, but I was strangely intrigued by it. Part of me wanted to see how far I could take it, peek a little bit further over the edge.

I went on a Spanish exchange in October and had a fantastic time, I was totally out of my comfort zone. I remember really enjoying all the food there; I had three meals a day and loved the new foods I was trying. The family I stayed with were lovely and ate really health-ily which made me feel good about myself, as was my exchange but I was still envious of her when she didn't have dinner. When I got back I was unwell and couldn't eat for a couple of days. I liked it, I liked how it made me look skinnier and I felt more independent and in control than ever. I'd never skipped meals before, but now things had changed, I felt like I'd cracked the secret and discovered it wasn't that hard.

Rachel and Rowena started asking questions, saying I looked thinner and that I seemed down. I avoided talking about it and made jokes or changed the subject. It was surprisingly easy to make light of feelings of helplessness, anxiety and inadequacy. My friends worried about things all the time, so it wasn't news if I was anxious. Sometimes I'd just pretend I didn't hear their words of genuine worry for my welfare. They asked Dan to talk to me and it shocked me that they cared enough to bring it up with him. When he asked me I felt like laughing. I knew I'd been feeling a bit down but I just had a lot going on at school, that was all.

I started going to the gym before work on Saturdays and when I had free periods at school. I'd get an uncontrollable sense of guilt if I didn't go at least three times a week. On Saturdays I would go to the gym before work, walk to work, have a banana on the way, and at lunchtime have a ryvita or pitta bread with a cup-a-soup. This may sound normal to you, but I used to look forward to lunch on a Saturday. I worked in a nice area of town with some of my favourite cafés around, and three months before this I would have chosen from jacket potatoes with chilli, or a Panini and a brownie, or a sandwich from the butchers. Not only was I very purposefully cutting out even the option of someone else compiling a meal for me, but also I was hiding the one I was making for myself.

The first half-term holiday we had from school I really started separating myself from people – a lot of the time to avoid eating, which I knew was awful but I couldn't stop it. I'd go out shopping, not for anything in particular just to leave the house and walk. At the shopping centre I only had a coffee for lunch. I was really proud of myself. I was starting to feel like I either ate and felt guilty and weak, or I could be alone and concentrate on work and feel in control. This was when I really started to notice my anxiety and fear towards food; I had to know when or what I was going to eat. I thought about it all the time. Different options of things I could have, and how much exercise I'd do to counteract it. The thoughts were consuming me completely.

As well as my A levels, I was taking on extra activities; we started a school charity and I took a lot of responsibility planning bake sales and other fundraisers, which I did really enjoy. No-one could grade me on my fund-raising skills, I didn't have to revise for a bake sale! However being the way I am it didn't help my anxieties about my workload and I started to feel more and more incapable. In Art and Drama in particular I felt I couldn't keep up with the rest of the class. I felt like they demanded personality, and mine was deteriorating drastically.

My family got a puppy at the beginning of December as my youngest sister's Christmas present, and we didn't really click. I didn't feel capable of loving her. She had so much energy and I just didn't. I was always tired, yet I couldn't relax and I felt very intimidated by the new member of the family – especially as she got so much attention from Mum and Dad. The puppy was so loving and happy; all I could do was snap at people because I was in such a ratty mood all the time.

In December, I really started feeling like Anorexia was taking over me. I was losing my sense of the fun, happy and sensible person I was and felt more lost and alone every day. I even got so worried I said to Ro and Rachel that I wanted to talk to them seriously about something but by the time we sat down to do it, the voices in my head had convinced me that I was fine and I didn't have a problem. *"You still eat all the time, and you're not technically underweight, are you?"* I'd say to myself. I weighed myself at the gym every time I went, checking the BMI chart above it to see where I was. To my dismay I was still on the edge of a "healthy" weight.

We stayed at Rachel's one night soon after that and Ro & I were sharing a bed. I started crying, I don't know why (I'd started doing that a lot too). Ro asked me what was wrong and I told her I thought I might have a problem.

"I can't stop obsessing about my weight. I've been losing weight and I like it. It makes me feel good but at the same scares me because I don't want to stop and get fat – why does that scare me so much? Am I that shallow?"

It was the first time I'd said any of this out loud to anyone, and the response I got really worried me.

"I know what you mean. And you want people to notice? Cos you're proud of doing it and looking skinny", Rowena replied. It scared me that she didn't seem that shocked or worried, and even more that she understood. I didn't want her to understand the hideous things this monster in my head was saying because I knew it was bad. I needed her to tell me this, not agree with them! I was so confused – I had no idea what was right and wrong any more. Was I just on a diet? Or did I have a real problem? When was I going to stop?

When I went home the next morning I found a book on my bed called "The Little Book of Self-Esteem" and inside it was a couple of pieces of paper. One had Mum's writing on and the other had mine. The one with mine on was from September time I think. I was worried about Ro because she'd stopped eating and I was feeling down, fat, ugly – as teenage girls do. I think I'd just needed to vent so wrote it down.

"I'm worried Rowena isn't eating, she's wasting away and there's nothing I can do. She makes me feel huge. I want to be 9 stone. I'm so big."

Then I read the note from Mum:

Dear Gracie,

I found this note in your bin ages ago and I kept it because it worried me. I get worried when I see you've lost weight and you don't admit it. You're thinner but still not happy. All of us who love you want you to love yourself, body and soul. I can't do it for you and we can't afford Gok for six weeks. It's not always easy. Everybody has bits of themselves (character as well as body) they're not very proud of. Some you can change and some you live with but try and keep it in proportion. You are lovely. Even if I wasn't your mum I would be proud to be your friend. You are also absolutely gorgeous physically and it's OK for you to see that.

Love always, Mumbasa x

I cried after reading it. Mainly because I was just as scared as her. I hadn't realised Mum and Dad had even noticed really. Obviously I thought I'd been hiding my behaviour better than in reality. I'd always been very mature and independent so they trusted me to look after myself. It was just this horrible thing in my head told me to abuse this trust and lie to them, which I hated. But I just couldn't find the strength to stop. I managed to just shrug it off and pretend everything was all right, even though my entire being knew it wasn't.

It made me sad that my mum was upset, but I already felt I couldn't change my eating habits. I was so used to it I'd feel disappointed if I "gave up". I felt that it would only make me sadder. I was feeling cold all the time and had the worst pins and needles, over and over, just from sitting still. I would just burst into tears sometimes, usually after or during work, or at social gatherings. I cried out of fear of failing or disappointing someone. I would always feel guilty after eating. Always.

The beginning

Liz

When did it start? When did I notice something was wrong?

I remember our holiday in Galicia at the beginning of August. It wasn't the best holiday in the world – not hot enough for lying around on the beach all day, which is what Grace & Emily, the older girls, wanted to do and was the point of going abroad rather than Wales. The sea was freezing, colder than Wales. There were a lot of mosquitoes. Ed and I were getting on each others' nerves. But it was that holiday that I looked back on later as 'normal' and "happy" for us all. Grace in her bikini, mucking about with Emily, helping Tilly to swim in the little pools, reading Mills & Boons wrapped in a sarong, hiding from the wind behind a rock. There was a Superromance we all three read and loved, 'The Last Honest Man'. Grace and Emily went to the local fiesta in the middle of the night and got chatted up by Manuel, the singer of one of the bands, all long curly hair and white jumpsuits. I heard a full account next morning, how he'd sung an impenetrable version of 'Grace Kelly' for her and she'd given him a fake phone number. They had clearly loved the whole experience.

In September G went into the sixth form. She was doing four subjects at AS level; and she started volunteering at a Special

School on Wednesday afternoon, and got involved with raising money for a school in Uganda, and on Saturdays she was working in a jewellery shop with her brother. She had been going out with Dan for about a year at this stage. She had joined a gym and was going regularly which again I thought was not a bad thing. Her father exercises a lot, and I thought it would be a balance for the intellectual demands of A-levels.

I can remember one day looking at her back view as she washed up, the grey baggy tracksuit, and saying *"You look thinner, have you lost weight?"* And instead of being pleased, her doing a sort of well, so what if I have? noise. It was off-key somehow. It threw me, because I didn't think it was bad for her to lose weight if she wanted to. I didn't want to over-react, or contradict her. I didn't think it was a bad thing, to learn that she could control her body shape to some extent. But her reaction was so odd, just not right. If she had been trying to lose weight, why was she not happy about me noticing? Why was she defensive? At one point during this school term, she said to me, *"I'm worried about Emily, I think she's not eating enough."* I thought that was odd. I had worries about her sister (as any mother of a teenager) but I hadn't worried about her eating.

I noticed Grace's sadness more than the thinness. I minded the sadness more than the thinness. She was very sad. She didn't smile, didn't join in with things, was distant. She seemed particularly down when she was with Dan, very subdued.

I didn't think about Deirdre. I knew they'd become distant and that Grace was quite relieved she had gone to another school, and I was pleased she was developing other friendships.

To start with, I tried asking her general questions, *"Are you OK?"* *"Is everything OK with Dan?"* She wouldn't say anything about it except, *"we're just really busy and don't see each other enough."*

I was worried enough to go to her and ask, *"What's on your mind? You seem very sad, and I'd like you to be able to talk to me."* Another time I asked specifically, *"Do you feel like things aren't right but you can't split up with Dan because everyone likes him?"*

I knew something was wrong. In November I knew she was sad. I didn't mind what shape or size she was as long as she was happy. Now, I don't think that I am someone who demands that my loved ones are happy all the time. I don't require a smile glued on – do I? Do I? I thought I made it clear that I loved them when they were sad as well, that it was OK and to have bad days and cry and get cross. But it seems not. Grace kept telling me she was fine, even when she obviously wasn't. I ask myself now, what was she scared of? What did she think would happen if she said, Look, I'm really not happy and things need to change?

At the beginning of December I found in the bin the crumpled notes that she had written – one that she had written about Rowena and how thin she was; one full of self-disgust about her body, and despair. I couldn't ignore them but didn't know what to do. So when I was in a bookshop I found the little book about self-esteem and left it for Grace in her room, with the notes and a letter to her. I thought if I said nice things to her she could just not listen, and dismiss them (because I am her mum), but if it was in writing she could read it in different moods and maybe it would go in at some level.

Towards Christmas *Grace*

The last week of term, Ro stopped eating so she'd look thin for the Christmas party. She'd been through phases of starving herself and had issues with food in the past but had been fine for about a year. I completely blamed myself. I really regretted talking to her about how I felt. On the last day we went swimming in our free periods and she commented on the gap I had between my thighs. I said I didn't like it. I grimaced and felt ashamed. *"Yeah, not nice"*, I said.

"You love it," she scorned. That made me so angry – I didn't want her to think I was like that! I hated wanting to be thin. I didn't think it made me any more attractive because of the ugly reasoning behind it. It wasn't who I was. But who was I without it?

I was feeling sad all the time in the week before Christmas. Sometimes I'd just burst into tears and I had panic attacks at least every two days. I'd be thinking about school or my family or Dan and I'd just get so scared, disappointed in myself. I wouldn't know what to do. I felt like I'd let down my family for letting anorexia take over me. My concentration was also getting a lot worse.

I was losing touch with everyone around me, especially Dan. Because I was always so lacking in energy and felt so pressured with schoolwork and going to the gym I didn't think I should be allowed to see him. And I also didn't think he should have to put up with me – why would he want to be around me? On Christmas Eve, all of my family had commented on my weight loss and that I wasn't eating enough. I remember trying to shrug it off with,

"I've only lost about half a stone."

"Whatever" (this was my brother). *"You used to have thighs."* They weren't having any of it.

I let myself have Christmas Day. I'd always said to myself I was allowed Christmas Day, whatever I wanted. I was truly happy for most of the day. I made the trifle, got loads of great presents from my family, and ate what I wanted to. I remember feeling content, happy and like myself but then after we'd had the trifle (which was fab, if I say so myself), I started to feel guilty. The voice in my head was telling me how disgusting I was for eating all of that food and not doing any exercise. I tried to make myself sick that night. This was when two serious truths hit home:

A) I had a real problem
B) Eating disorders don't celebrate Christmas.

On Boxing Day I was really confused; I didn't know what the rules were any more. I'd said I'd stop dieting at Christmas, but I couldn't remember how to eat normally. I'd fantasised about not being on a diet, about preparing a meal and eating it, about sandwiches, muesli, spag bol, ice cream and now I was meant to be allowed them – why? When? How? I was worried that if I started eating I wouldn't stop because I was so hungry. And then I'd get fat. And then I wouldn't be 'pretty, thin Grace' any more. I'd not be what people expected me to be, and they'd lose interest and stop talking to me, and then what would I have?? I felt so scared it really was all I could think about.

New Year

Grace

I spent that New Year's Eve with Dan, standing in the hallway of some student party, feeling like a spare part because I was so upset. I found it so hard to bring out some personality to talk to people. It felt like all of my simple, happy and friendly emotions were buried under miles of heavy, ugly complications clear as mud. I thought I couldn't feel any worse but then I bumped into Deirdre for the first time in months. I went back to Dan's and felt really sad. We ate a pizza and I felt guilty.

On New Year's Day I felt awful, really down, and had tummy ache. I didn't eat anything at all, all day.

The following days after that, I spent mainly at home, pretending to have breakfast, going to the gym, and doing school work.

One of those mornings, I was sitting in the dining room doing some Spanish revision and my Dad came in and sat down next to me, closing the door behind him.

"Hi love," he said. *"Me and Mum are really worried about you. Your mum cries every night. Why haven't you been eating?"*

This hit me really hard, because Dad and I never had proper serious talks.

"I think I've got a problem." That was the first time I said it out loud at home. I started crying and Dad tried to reassure me.

"I'm sorry, I don't know what to say to make things better. Mum's better at this kind of thing," he said. At least he could still make me smile. We agreed I should see the family doctor.

That night I talked to Mum. It was so scary to see her crying, and so worried. It was even worse because it was my fault. I'd done that to her. She seemed so vulnerable, like I'd never seen her before. I thought she was over-reacting though - it's not like I had a proper eating disorder. After all I wasn't even underweight... I felt like I had to reassure her and look after her. I felt guilty for how she felt and her pain. *"I'm not worth it,"* I thought.

We went to the GP the next day. It was a lady I hadn't met before. She got me to fill in a questionnaire about some of my feelings, and that showed I was clinically depressed. However, when it came to my other feelings, she was a lot less helpful.

"Well, it definitely seems like you have an eating disorder," she said. Then she weighed me, and said I wasn't technically underweight. This made the voice in my head laugh – it mocked me. *"What kind of an anorexic are you?! Must try harder!"*

After this I was just as confused as before. It was comforting to know what was wrong with me, but the GP didn't seem too worried and just told us to try and have breakfast together and come back next week. I knew I wanted to get better, for my family now, but I also wanted to be underweight. When we came back from the doctor I cried in the bathroom, my sister Emily on the other side of the door trying to comfort me. I felt so far away from her, I couldn't remember the last time I'd even spoken to her.

The following week of enforced breakfasts was absolute agony. I would cry over a bowl of muesli or a bagel, feeling helpless and awful. I told Rachel and Rowena, and my form tutor. He was really supportive and made it clear that if I needed anything he was there for me, and nothing was more important than my health. It felt nice to share some of the burden. Ro and Rachel weren't really surprised. They knew enough, they didn't need a label for it.

The next week we went back and saw the same doctor. She weighed me and I'd lost more weight. Apart from that, she didn't tell us anything. Apparently I was being referred to a specialist, who was on holiday or training, and we were also being referred to the Eating Disorder Service, which was taking a while. She seemed to have the approach that we wanted to book a holiday, not get some treatment for a traumatic mental illness.

In January, we had our work's late Christmas meal at my brother Seth's favourite Italian restaurant. I ordered a bowl of pasta and pushed it around my plate for half an hour, urging myself to take a bite but I physically couldn't. I felt like crying. Seth was sat next to me and he smiled sympathetically. I hadn't told him that I'd been diagnosed but I'm sure he knew enough. It was so hard to sit there and pretend nothing was wrong. I just wanted the world to dissolve, for Seth to hug me and tell me everything would be all right. I stayed at Rachel's that night and was feeling really down. I started to cry while we were watching TV and managed to actually talk about what was upsetting me. I told her and Rowena about how I felt so guilty and helpless, because I knew I was hurting my family so much but there was no way I could stop it. I felt better after talking, but the voice in my head wanted me to stay sad, not to enjoy happiness or my friend's support. As we were going to sleep that night I was on a mattress on the floor and they were in bed. I heard Ro saying to Rachel, *"I hate anorexia. I wish it was a person so I could kill it and rip its head off."*

At the time I couldn't see why they cared so much and why they were putting up with me – but now I see they weren't "making do" or "putting up" with anything – they were just being my friends and looking out for me, just as usual.

The following day I worked in the jewellery shop. Mum took me to the deli next door for lunch and I had half a Panini. She looked sad afterwards and I took it as her being disappointed in me.

The following Saturday, there was just me and Seth working in the shop. We hardly talked all day and I spent most of it huddled over the heater in the back room because I was so cold. He texted me that night saying how worried he was, and I told him I'd talk to him properly tomorrow. When I told him about it he said, *"I thought that was it."* We lay on my bed and he just hugged me, I felt truly safe. After a while he asked me, *"When you've got a plate of food and you're thinking, 'Wow, this looks really nice, I'm gonna eat all of it...'"*

"I don't think that!" I said, as if trying to prove a point that my anorexia was serious and real. For me to admit that I was going to eat an entire plate of food felt like admitting I was a rabbit. It was and never would be true to me.

"OK", he continued slowly, *"but what would you feel if you did eat it?"*

"That I'd have to go to the gym afterwards and work it off." He then told me that's stupid, and explained the logic of calories and GDA and stuff – but I told him it made no difference to how I felt about food. He then told me he went through the same thing last year when he was having a bad time with a girlfriend – this made me hopeful that if he could beat this disgusting thing I could too. But this thought was counteracted by a thousand negative ones, *"You're not even good at losing weight – why put it back on? What about all the effort you put in? You'll just go back to being fat and dumpy."*

Some time in January, my Spanish exchange Ana came to stay, and because I was feeling so down it was harder to be around her and make the effort to socialise. Meal times were really hard. Mum and Dad tried to act like everything was fine – they'd always say, *"You sure you've had enough?"* when I left most of my food. Sometimes they'd say, *"Please try and have some more."* That used to make me SO angry – I'd think that they thought I wasn't putting enough effort in – that I was starving myself for the sake of it – like I could just switch it on and off. I tried to explain to Ana that I wasn't very well, but it's hard to know how much she understood.

At this point I was hardly speaking to my sister Emily – we lived in parallel with each other and never seemed to meet. We'd go to school together in the mornings but it was like we were in separate impenetrable bubbles. We'd exchange words – it's not like we fell out – we just lost touch. It felt like there was so much we avoided talking about it, it was always like walking on eggshells – everyone was afraid of saying what they wanted to.

We carried on going to see the GP weekly and referrals were being slow. We went to the self-help group, SYEDA, Mum and me, and talked to Laura. The building it was based in was ignorable from the outside, hidden behind a library. But inside it was lovely, and warm. Laura showed us round and explained who they were and what they did, for the first time I wasn't made to feel guilty for what was happening to me. I was able to tell Mum that I thought she should talk to someone there because I couldn't deal with it on my own, I couldn't bear to listen to how her heart was breaking. It was such a relief to say that and know that she and Dad had support.

The Friday of Ana's stay I came home from school early, because I was really tired and felt so down. Dad was at home when I got back and I cried on him for about an hour.

"What's wrong? I don't understand, love. Why don't you let yourself eat?"

"I don't deserve it. I'm not a good person. I don't do any-thing. I'm not likeable," I said, through a nose full of snot.

"Of course you're likeable, don't be ridiculous. Everyone loves you. I don't understand why you can't see that, darling."

That night, me and Ana went to a party. I remember having a sip of something sugary and blue, it tasted great and instantly went to my head. I thought maybe this could be an option for when I felt really bad, as a pick-me-up. I took it home in my bag thinking I could just drink if I was sad, but I knew how many calories were in it and never touched it again. We stayed just long enough I think, and when we got back I went and sat in the living room with Dad. He was crying; this scared me more than anything. I'd only ever seen my dad cry once (when Seth and my cousin Harry broke some trees at a campsite and shamed the family).

His eyes were small and red, and he wasn't looking at me as I perched on the side of the sofa, fear swimming around my head.

"You used to sing in the kitchen when you were making your breakfast, and it would drive me crazy. It would annoy me so much I'd just think 'SHUT UP!' But now I'd give anything to hear you sing again."

It broke my heart to hear that. It was like a ton of bricks landed in my stomach. The guilt I felt then was the worst ever, seeing my Dad in so much pain. I completely blamed myself.

"Me and Mum don't know what to do, Grace. Mum cries every night. I can't stand watching you waste away like this."

"I'm sorry, Dad, I'm so sorry. I'm gonna get better. I know I will, I'll try harder for you."

"I won't let this kill you, even if I have to sit and watch you cry over a plate of rice for hours on end. I won't let you die."

New Year   *Liz*

I was so pleased that Grace ate properly over Christmas and
seemed to enjoy herself. But she was definitely too thin
and I knew from the stocks in the bathroom cabinet that
she had not had a period for a while. After Christmas our
relatives went home and her mood went downhill again.

On New Year's Day we were at home and at lunch time Grace
would not eat anything except a few mouthfuls of salad. She came
down stairs clutching a hot water bottle to her stomach and said
she wasn't very hungry. She then said she had period pains. I did
not respond verbally or do anything but I felt a rush of alarm and
adrenalin shoot through me. Because I knew this was a lie, and for
Grace to lie to me was very, very unusual. I was scared because I
suddenly knew that something was taking over my lovely daughter.

I'd had the ghost words *"anorexia nervosa"* fluttering around at
the edge of my consciousness for a little while but did not want
to pin a label onto what was happening with Grace. I didn't
know what was cause and what was effect, the thin-ness, the
despondency, the detachment from life and loving. I didn't know
if her distance from Dan was because she didn't like him any
more and didn't know how to break it off, or if it was because
she hated herself and thought he was stupid for loving her.

On January 3rd I had to work but Ed was at home with Grace, and he sat down with her and talked to her about her not eating. He said she seemed relieved to talk about it, and later she said *"I thought, if my dad has noticed then maybe there really is something wrong."* He was hoping work would be snowed off but he had to go in at 5. Grace agreed to come to the doctor's with me the next day. She was going to meet me there – it's only 10 minutes' walk from home.

Text from Ed (04/01/08):
I think it might be better if you picked her up. She's fallen asleep.

The visit to the doctor was odd. It was such a big step for Grace to admit she had a problem and was ready to see a doctor that maybe I was over-optimistic. The doctor said that Grace was depressed but seemed to think that because her BMI was just within the normal range there was no urgency. But she said she would look at referrals and made us an appointment for the following week.

Text from Dan (late that evening):
If there's anything I can do or you and E need any-thing from me don't hesitate to let me know. At the same time if you ever want me to back off or

anything please tell me. I know its up to g but
I don't want you to feel im interfering or getting in the way. Thanks a lot. Hope youre ok.

The next day I met Grace at work and took her to the café
next door for lunch. She ate half a Panini. I would have
liked her to eat more but did not push it. I didn't realise
at the time that there would be weeks when I looked back
on her eating half a Panini at lunchtime with nostalgia.

Now that the problem had been named, it got worse day by day. It
is almost getting hard to remember just how awful it was. The sitting in front of a plate of food with Grace crying silently, maybe
cutting things up and moving them around the plate. Sometimes
she would even take a mouthful and then dissolve again. She
would look as though she was in pain, and cry, and say, *"I'm so
sorry. I just can't, don't ask me to."*

Text to Ed (10/01/08):
Grace has hardly eaten anything and Em is crying.
Zelda (the dog) has chewed Grace's shoes and Tilly is
eating custard out of a jug. I an looking forward to
you coming home!

That sums up our life for a while. Everybody coping in their own
way and just about getting by. On Saturday Seth and Grace were

working at the shop and I dropped off some football boots Seth had left at our house.

Text from Seth (Saturday 12/01/08):
Hey ma thanks for bringing over those boots. Well beyond the call of motherly duty. Am I being neurotic or has anyone else noticed graces complete lack of appetite. She ate about 3 mouthfuls of her £7 spaghetti last night (they'd been out for a work do) and about 2 mouthfuls of those sandwiches (when delivering the boots I had taken her some lunch). she has hardly said a word all day.

Reply to Seth:
Yes, talk to her. The doctor has referred her to an eating disorder clinic but day to day she is eating almost nothing. She is very depressed and I am really worried. I an glad that you have noticed, I thought she would talk to you today x

I emailed my sister Mel, who's a nurse, and has had postnatal depression. I felt she would understand.

Sent: Sunday, January 20, 2008 6:17 PM
Subject: Help please

Hi there - hope you had a good Christmas and New Year & I promise Finn will have a birth-day present by the end of the week!

Grace is having a really rough time at the moment and I just wondered with your knowledge of the Health Service and depression you had anything to suggest. I realised before Christmas that she was feeling low and getting thin - but she's always ill in December and it was a long school term. She was OK on Christmas Day but by New Year I was really worried since she has almost completely stopped eating. She agreed to come to the doctor's with me and has talked to me and Ed separately at length about how down she is and how it seemed to be taking over. She has gone beyond self-help.

The doctor has seen Grace 3 Fridays in a row and referred her to an eating disorder clinic and a coun-sellor and neither referral has come through. After a brief chat and weighing (She is under 8.5 stone now and nearly 5ft 10) the doctor said she thought G was extremely depressed (duh) and needed medica-tion which she as a GP did not have the expertise to prescribe so she ought to see a specialist. I think this is a good idea because you do need to be very careful with anti-depressants especially in a young malnourished person. When I asked about timescale she said they would make an effort to see her in a few weeks - which is just not good enough. I had already said about how it is getting worse more quickly and I want something to happen now. So then she gave me the option of paying - if I'd had my wits about me I would have sent G out of the room because she will now worry about money and what we're spend-ing on her. So I think I have agreed to pay for a private consultation but don't know if that means everything has to be paid for - medication etc.

The thing that did make me angry was that I men-tioned incidentally about the contraceptive implant G had put in in October - and the doctor looked it up IN A BOOK SHE HAD ON HER DESK and said "Oh yes, depression can be a side-effect"!!! She has had Grace's notes out at least three times and that was the thing immediately before this problem. But she doesn't do these implants so we have to book with another doctor at the practice to get it removed but we could have done that a fortnight ago if some-one had put two and two together. I doubt the whole cause is as simple as that but ANY contributing factor has got to be removed. I only thought of it because Ed's sister had mentioned she's needed anti-depressants since starting the menopause. And me not sitting and making her eat is not working for either of us, so I will start eating with her again.

Anyway... our outing to High School Musical on Ice was absolutely ace and the best thing was that Grace LOVED it. She was her old self, smiling & animated, and voluntarily went to the fridge and ate a yogurt when we came home. It was such a relief. I got through most of Friday without crying!

If you can offer any suggestions about how to progress - preferably without paying a for-tune but I will if necessary. As I said to Grace, I will cook her Christmas dinner every day if it will tempt her to eat again.

Love to all of you,
Liz

The next day, I took the morning off work and went to the doctor myself. I saw one of the partners who has treated our family for several years, and initially I asked for a prescription for acne cream. Then I asked her if she could follow up these referrals for Grace which weren't happening, and I cried and tried to explain my frustration when I could see her fading away in front of my eyes and people were saying "a few weeks" as though that was perfectly reasonable.

The GP was great, and offered me anti-depressants, which I refused because I said I thought the way I was reacting was perfectly reasonable in the circumstances and I was still functioning. She was fine with this and immediately put things in motion to try to get specialist help for Grace quickly. Her secretary was an absolute godsend, and would ring me every day to tell me how far she had got with the various avenues, even when there was nothing to report. She would ring and say things like "*I finish work at 2.30 today but I wanted you to know I've left another message with so-and-so. They haven't got back to me, but I'll ring and chase it again tomorrow.*" It was incredibly comforting for me that she did this, because I felt that someone else was taking it seriously and cared about my daughter.

She gave me the number of SYEDA (the South Yorkshire Eating Disorders Association) on Tuesday and I rang and talked to the person who answered the phone. It was brilliant to have someone listening with some understanding. She said it was good that Grace was in two minds, that she did have at least some part that wanted to get better. I realised when she said it, that some parents have to watch their children fade away while telling them that nothing is wrong.

Text to G (22/01/08):
hey sweetie I have got an appointment at a clinic on thurs morning for us both. It's 9.30.

Text to G (23/01/08):
hey babe how are you? the nice secretary rang and the clinic has accepted your referral and will see you within the month. So quicker than the private bod who hasn't got spaces till april. Love you, mum x

Two days later we went to SYEDA for the first time. The meeting surprised me on several levels:

a) That it existed, but that some GPs weren't aware of it.

b) That the building was so nice – they had had a great donation from Next Home, more stuff than they could use.

c) That they asked me to refer myself separately, and made it clear that the organisation was there to support carers as well as sufferers. The approach that carers can be helped and can actually feel better, even if their loved one is denying the problem and possibly not getting better, was startling. Grace and I sat at an angle to each other, quite separate, and Grace said, *"Yes, please, I want you to do this. I can't cope when you tell me how upset you are."* She seemed relieved to have been able to say this. Part of me bristled, thinking, *"You're not the only one who can't cope. I can't pretend I'm all right any more because I'm really not."* But it was the first time for weeks that she had voluntarily come out with something spontaneous and energetic-sounding and I could see that it was important. I had said I'd do anything, hadn't I? So if it helped her for me not to offload how much I was hurting, I had to do that and SYEDA offered other people who would listen.

Text to E (24/01/08):
grace liked the woman and trusted her. She will go on her own next Wed and me on 4th feb.

I had a helpful response from my sister:

Subject: Re: Help please
Date: Thu, January 24, 2008 11:37 am

Hi Liz,

Thanks for getting in touch, don't know if I was much help but hopefully things are improving now you are in touch with the self help group. I would suggest they are the best people to assist as they are specialists in the area and should cover

all aspects eg psychiatric, physical and family/
emotional, hopefully without the use of drugs.

It sounds very much like you need to cherry
pick your appointments with the 2nd GP, they
sound far more in touch with the real world!

I know the most important thing at the moment is
helping and supporting Grace, but please make sure
you look after yourself too. If there was 1 thing I
came away from my counselling sessions realising, it
was that you need to have a bit of me time or you're
no use to anyone. Even if that just means a glass
of wine and good book while soaking in the bath for
an hour. At least you can lock the door in there!

I hope the session went well today and you
all feel a bit more positive and that there
is help out there. Really looking forward
to seeing you all in a couple of weeks.

Loads of love to you all

Mxx

February

January turned into February. One of things SYEDA offered was massage and I went to try and relax, to help me sleep. I didn't enjoy it. I hated being touched, even in a nice way. It just made my skin crawl. All I could think about was how I'd avoid having tea, and I was still cold despite the heating being on and the warm feel of the oils. There was still a voice in my head that told me not to relax as well. I felt I didn't deserve it.

That weekend my favourite auntie came to stay for "second Christmas". I made trifle, and I ate a bowl of it! Rachel congratulated me for it on the Monday after – and I felt awful, like I'd cheated. It was strange seeing my Auntie and cousin, they were our closest extended family and my cousin has always been like a brother to me. But when I saw him, I couldn't think of a thing to say. There was nothing that I could remember he'd been doing, or anything I was interested in that I thought he'd like. It was like we were strangers. We spent most of the day together and I still don't know if we had a conversation. That evening after dinner, I was sat in the living room watching TV and my Auntie came and sat next to me. I was drinking hot water, and she said *"Would you like some tea or* coffee? I could just put some milk in there?" I gave her the look that said, "Come one, we all know I'm not going to do that. I can't. I don't want to. It doesn't matter anyway." That was also the weekend when I scalded my hand whilst trying to make a hot water bottle, I was so tired that I poured hot water straight from the kettle onto the hand that was holding the spout of the hot water bottle. The pain was excruciating, it carried on burning all through the night.

Rachel and Rowena were making a special effort – I could see they were trying, a lot of the time I avoided them because I wanted to forget about anorexia, pretend it didn't exist and just get on with life. I was so terrified of confronting it. They were the only people I talked openly with about it and I felt like that added such a weight to our relationship. They told me that people were asking questions at school, and asked if they were allowed to explain the situation. I said they couldn't, I didn't want everyone knowing I was crazy. It's not like other people cared, they were just being nosy and would judge me. Or so I thought.

Dan had wanted to take me to Paris for ages and it was due to happen at Valentine's – but one night after another failed family meal, Mum and I decided I wasn't well enough and should go away with the family to North Yorkshire instead. I lay on my bed and cried, feeling all kinds of disappointment. When I rang Dan to tell him between sobs, he sounded let down. But said that it was okay. It didn't feel okay.

The night before we went to Dent in North Yorkshire, I wet the bed. At the age of 16, I wet the bed, because I didn't have the physical ability or strength to get out of bed and go to the loo. Most nights I would lie, wrapped in clothes, blankets and a hot water bottle not sleeping. For all of the cold, hunger and sadness I couldn't sleep. And when I did, I'd wake with a start and feel cheated. A lot like with my eating behaviour, I felt I didn't deserve sleep. That particular night I was somewhere in between sleep and consciousness, drifting in and out of my blurry exist-ence. I was aware of it happening, but felt so heavy with cold and sadness and apathy that I didn't move. *"Just get through the night"* I thought. Did the bed-wetting make me change my ways? No. The next day I changed my sheets, threw away the pyjamas I'd soiled, and spent the day walking around town, buying diet coke and avoiding eating. I felt so ashamed of myself. I was just so disap-pointed and humiliated. What was I?!

That week away was one of the hardest. I cried most of the way there. That week me, Rachel and Ro had planned to live at my house before I went to Paris, and we had really looked forward to it, and I felt like I'd let them down.

We stayed in a renovated youth hostel with all of my aunties and their young children. I spent most of my time hiding in my room, or in the drying room to keep warm. Something prompted me to try a boiled egg – a magazine article I think. I remember when I finished it I was ecstatic! I went and showed the empty egg-shell to Dad and he asked, "Did you eat it?"

I grinned and nodded, "Yeah."

And then he hugged me. I felt so proud of myself, which was such a nice change from feeling guilty. The house was in the middle of nowhere – in fact it was further away than the middle of nowhere. I'd go on stupidly long, angry walks and dream about jumping on a train and going anywhere but back to the house. I wrote a letter to Emily that week, thanking her and apologising for everything, and I got a wonderful love-filled reply.

The weekend after we got back, I stayed at Rachel's. We went for a walk around Mayfield Valley and for some reason I bought some Quorn sausages. She didn't ask any questions or laugh at me – just let me do it. I ate two of them! Rachel's house was really the only place I felt safe – I could just "be" when I was there.

February

Since our first visit to SYEDA I had gone for a session on my own – it was a chance to express my helplessness and frustration and to talk to someone who listened very calmly and felt no need to say, *"Oh, you poor thing. How awful!"* It was very calm and serious, just what I needed. I did not say anything to any of my work colleagues at this stage – because sympathy would have been the last straw. While at work I could try to switch off and concentrate on something else. But I missed a couple of important deadlines, and on one occasion completely forgot to pick up Tilly from after-school club. Cutting my work life off completely from home life did not work entirely; but it was the only way I could work at all. I have always had a ridiculously good memory; I can recite the number plates of every car my family has owned since 1967. But on one of those days some students were washing cars for charity in our work car park – and I couldn't remember my own, current, registration number.

I read a lot on the internet and borrowed a book from SYEDA which gave me some ideas about how to talk to Grace. I wasn't sure if it would help, but I knew that because we lived with her day in, day out, we had to find some way of surviving. Having some suggestions of how to go about living with someone with an eating disorder, to get past the endless circular arguments and the fruitless confrontation, was helpful. Should we try to make her eat? Try to eat with her? Enforce it?

The first Tuesday of February we went to a SYEDA support group. I asked Ed if he would come, desperately hoping he would, thinking he probably wouldn't, trying not to show my desperation. He came with me. That in itself was incredible support for me. The meeting was interesting and it was a relief to be with people who understood, but I cannot say that it was cheering. There was a parent there whose child had recovered from anorexia within a year and was now eating and feeling positive; there was another parent whose child was still battling at the age of 39, 25 years after the onset of the disease. We heard about the NHS residential unit in Leeds (Leeds - over an hour away!). There was a private residential clinic in Sheffield but the only person who had experience of being referred there lived in Rotherham. There was a lot of frustration with the health service from people who had been battling far longer than us. Everyone said, you as the carer will have to nag, and fight, and plead, otherwise nothing will happen.

February half-term approached. Dan had asked me – when? I can't remember - whether it would be OK to ask Grace to come to Paris with him. It was quite touching – there was a school trip to Paris with the Art department later in the year but he wanted to be the person who showed her Paris for the first time. It was nice that he asked if we would be happy about it. My hesitation was that I wasn't sure if Grace would really want to go.

We had a holiday house booked with my three sisters and by mid-January I knew I couldn't let Grace go abroad, that I couldn't let Dan have the responsibility of looking after her when she was so fragile. So I told them that I wanted G to come with us. I thought about not going but on balance decided some time away would do us good and that nothing about Grace's illness would change in a different location.

We had heard nothing from the Eating Disorder Service so, spurred on by the support group, I rang them and asked when Grace would be seen.

Text to G (08/02/08):
Hey babe they say your appointment will prob be 4th March. I moaned a bit and they said if there was a cancellation they'd see you sooner. Can you make sure there are boots and boats or even coats* for everyone and pile them by the front door? Thank you, see you later love mumbasa.

(*boats was the first guess of predictive text)

The week away was painful, but the pain would have been there at home too; being right away from work, in the hills, we took time out. One day Ed and I walked up Whernside with my brother-in-law and the dog: a beautiful crisp day with snow under the walls and ice on the puddles but bright sun. Eleven miles hard going, good for the soul. And there were moments of brightness involving Grace, too – a game of pool, blondes versus brunettes, one evening; the afternoon she ate a boiled egg. Most of the time, though, she cried in her bedroom, and cried in the drying room. (Youth Hostel drying rooms - always warm. They will probably be banned soon as being un-carbon-friendly, but what a fantastic institution.) She had pleaded with me, don't make me eat at the table with all the little kids, so I'd set up a table and chair in the drying room, where I would take her miniscule portion of food and sit with her. I would try and let her know that I still loved her, that my wanting her to eat was not to punish her; that I saw anorexia as a separate thing that was her enemy, our enemy.

Despite eating almost nothing Grace was still strong. She had a well of anger inside her which seemed to give her strength. She came out walking with me but strode off ahead so that I couldn't keep up. She did not want to talk or even be with me. I had to get back to the house to cook tea, and had to shout at her receding back, trusting that she would choose to come back to the place she obviously hated, not get lost, not be out in the dark. She did come back.

We got back from Dent on the 15th, to find Grace had an appointment on the 19th at the Eating Disorder Service (a branch of the NHS based at the Community Mental Health Hospital). I had to take time off work so it was necessary to explain to my boss. She was remarkably understanding, considering her famous intolerance of absence or any sign of human frailty.

To: Ed
From: Liz
Date: 19/02/08

The appointment seemed to go OK this morning – I went in and saw the lady at the end. She said it will take a couple of appointments to sort out a care plan and she will talk to her colleagues in a team meeting. She seems quite worried about how much G is doing as well as how little she's eating. Talk properly later x

To: Liz
From: Ed
Date: 19/02/08

Thanks for the update. I know it's upsetting but we should at least be pleased they are taking it seriously and are discussing in team meetings etc. I have been worried all year that she is not eating enough to get her through a day at school? Perhaps a break would be good?

The matrons have been out for chicken and chips and the smell is overpowering. It's like the concept of healthy eating never reached the third floor of Bailey House. Haven't had my sardines yet. Starving.

Keep your chin up. See you later.

Love

To: Ed
From: Liz
Date: 21/02/08

Morning. How are you? Zelda was definitely a bit mental this morning and appeared to be starving - not impressed with Bakers Complete. She had my sandwich off the side while my back was turned and ate half of it - despite the fact that it was marmite & cucumber which I wouldn't have thought was doggy-licious.

I looked for worm stuff on the internet and it looks like you have to get it from the vet so I'll book her in for a vet session tomorrow or next week. A friend at work says they charge about £21 for worm treatment - five drops on the back of the neck!! However, after all that sheep poo it's probably a good idea. See you later Love Liz

To: Liz
From: Ed
Date: 21/02/08

Hi. She seemed Ok with Winalot. Thanks for the update anyway. Sorry I was grumpy this morning. I am really, really stressed out about Grace and I am trying to be normal for everyone else (as I know you are too) and I am finding it hard to rein everything in. I nearly burst into tears on Valley Road this morning.

I'm feeling better now. Had a cup of tea and am doing an Open Learning pack on employment legislation. Probably have another cup of tea soon.

Love you.

Ed

Hi. Hope your day is OK. Employment legislation sounds more interesting than dormant filing, I have to say. I didn't realise you were so upset about Grace. We've not really talked about it since the hol. I am quite grateful for the demands of my job but I cope by locking myself into a work mindset which leads to things like forgetting Tilly. The one-to-one counselling at SYEDA is something you could do as well but you have to go and refer yourself. The phone number is 2728822. It's just good to talk to someone who understands. I talked to my boss yesterday and she has a friend with a daughter in a very similar position - a community psychiatric nurse was very helpful for her. I don't really feel like telling anyone else at work, especially since one lady found out on Monday her husband has lung cancer, so that is really bad news. I have defrosted some chicken so will prob make a curry or stirfry or something.

Liz

Day is still going ok thanks. I think I'm a bit of an ostrich with the Grace situation - it's the only way I can get through the day. And I know that you are really engaged with it and stressed out by it so I don't want to make things any more stressful for you. i don't think I need any more support than what I get from you.

Something weird happening with the alignment of this email. Stir fry/curry sounds good. I'll have mine when I get back from my run.

When our lives are on a more even keel I think we should look seriously into moving to the countryside.

Love Ed

To: Liz
From: Ed
Date: 22/02/08

Morning love. Let us know how it went at school this morning when you can.

And so begins another weary day...

Ed

xxx

To: Ed
From: Liz
Date: 22/02/08

Hi love

It was good to meet Mrs Callaghan (head of 6th form) and Mr Wilson (Drama) who is Grace's form teacher and confidant. They obviously have experience of several students going through different hard times and want to support her. We talked about giving her some structure without putting pressure on her - e.g. she could go and do some sewing in the Textiles room and use their overlocker (something she said yesterday she would like to do) - but it wouldn't be a set time-table & she wouldn't be letting anyone down if she didn't feel like it.   We agreed that we needed to see how it went with her remaining two subjects: they are happy for her to opt in and out as she likes; they will keep her entered for the exams for the time being.

Mr W also said that if Grace agrees to start drinking the build-up drinks he would be happy to keep her company while she has her lunchtime prescription, which is nice. He would also like to keep her involved very casually with drama (e.g. just watching stuff and making comments). I didn't really know how to stop other students making crass comments but I did ask them to make teachers aware of what is actually going on because that will stop them doing something inappropriate by accident e.g. commenting on appearance, talking about food, etc., speculating that she has cancer etc. I think simple, accurate information will stop some rumours. Basically I just asked school to keep being calm and consistent and trying to keep things normal as far as possible, but I know that there are people watching out for her who will realise she is not feeling normal at all.

The head teacher sent a message of support. I might send him an email just to say thank you & make contact. See you later. Love L

Liz

To: Ed

From: Liz

Date: 21/02/08

Hi love

Thanks for the update. Sounds like a useful meeting. It's good to know G has teachers looking out for her. When can she start on the build-up drinks? Is it something she has to agree to?

Ed

xxx

To: J Howard (Staff)
From: Liz
Date: 25/02/08

Dear Mr Howard

I just wanted to say thank you for the message you passed on via the staff I talked to last week. There wasn't anything we discussed that I would not want you to be party to; I am glad the school is happy to keep Grace registered on a reduced timetable for as long as she feels able to attend. I would like the relevant staff to know precisely what the matter is. As I said to them, I think some limited accurate information will stop ill-informed speculation. Grace has anorexia. She is eating very, very little and may well have to be hospitalised within weeks. It is a strange and powerful disease and turns you into a different person. She is very depressed and has very low self-esteem. She gets very anxious and withdrawn around conversations about food, appearance, body image, etc. If anyone is interested in more information the SYEDA website is very good

www.syeda.org.uk

I don't think there's any way of stopping students being insensitive: probably not, and Grace will have to develop standard conversation-stoppers if she doesn't want to answer questions. It is good to keep engaging her in activities outside herself and her own obsessions (so I think both Spanish and Politics which depend on debate and conversation are healthier than Art which can be unending, solitary

and obsessive). Surrounding her with a calm, consistent, supportive environment and leaving the probing and challenging to others is the best way to go, I think.

Thanks for your support,

Liz

To: Liz
From: J Howard (Staff)
Date: 25/02/08

Dear Liz

I was glad to receive your message this afternoon.

Please be re-assured that we at GHS will do all we can to support Grace. We will be flexible and patient and not lose hope. Whatever else is going on in Grace's mind, she should not fear any rejection or criticism from the School. We will be guided by you about what is best.

If you would wish us to explain to Grace's friends at some stage, then we will do that but please feel that you can pick up the phone or send an email at any time. It goes without saying that if you want to contact me out of hours, then you must not hesitate.

Jim Howard

Headteacher

I was gradually opening up to people and sharing our situation. I was not surprised that there was a lot of love out there for Grace but I never quite knew what to say. *"How did that happen?"* people would ask. *"But she's so beautiful."* This is absolutely true – no maternal bias whatever.

I felt weary at the thought of trying to explain, defensive in case they jumped to conclusions about her, and us. I couldn't help feeling that it was our fault in some way and that other people would think that too.

Dan passed on his parents' good wishes and I tried to describe what was happening.

To: R.henderson37@yahoo.co.uk
From: Liz

Dear Bob

Thank you for your message of support – yes, Grace has anorexia and is very weak. She is also very depressed and seems to have gone beyond being able to help herself.

Dan continues to be lovely. I don't know if their relationship will survive but she does seem to be able to be happy with him sometimes and he seems to want to be with her even when she is despondent. One of the things about low self-esteem is that you lose respect for people who think you're nice & beautiful so that is a very hard thing to deal with.

I did wonder if the relationship was an added pressure (what will happen when he goes away? what will happen if we stay together and I never go out with anyone else?) but I see him as part of the solution rather than the problem and appreciate him talking to me. I know you and Jocelyn are fond of Grace, and vice versa. Do keep in touch. Best wishes

Liz

To: Liz
From: R Henderson

Dear Liz

I wasn't sure if it was appropriate to get in touch but wanted you to know we are thinking of you. Of course Grace has become special to us as a family. We are very fond of her - she is an exceptional and lovely girl. We share with you the worries and fears you must have at the moment. If there is anything we can do to help, please let us know.

Dan is coping as best he can. he does not seem able to talk about Grace and her illness to us and we try hard not to put him under pressure. He will not see your message unless you want him to. We do not know how much he knows about anorexia and about what Grace may yet have to face.

As for their relationship, I think Dan feels a sense of protective loyalty to Grace. Who knows what the long term holds but he cares deeply about her and understands at least some of her vulnerability.

Please convey to Grace in whatever way may be appropriate our feelings of affection for her and that for us she is still the lovely girl we have got to know over the last 18 months or so.

With kindest regards

Bob (& Jocelyn) Henderson

To: Ed
From: Liz
Date: 26/02/08

Hi love.

Very sweet email from Dan's dad attached.

The appointment this morning made her very angry and upset. She has a prescription for buildup drinks (part of the cause of the rage) which I am going to Boots to fetch with her after school. Hoping to do 4.45 leave work 5.00 meet G at Boots 5.20 pick up Zelda 5.30 pick up Tilly & take Zelda to vets for 5.45. There is stock and lots of veg around for soup. Or we could have pitta bread & houmous and salad. Emily is dancing till 8 so it is we 3 again. Love Liz

Liz

To: Liz
From: Ed
Date: 26/02/08

Hi

Thanks. Why is she upset about the drinks? Does she not want to get better? I am getting rageous myself.

Nice note from Dan's dad. Don't care what we have for supper.

Ed

To: Liz
From: Ed
Date: 26/02/08

Hi

Sorry I snapped at you earlier. I am completely stressed out. Poor old Tilly - I shouted at her and made her cry. It is really Grace I want to shout at. The dog somehow jumped up and ate my sandwiches. I am permanently on the verge of tears.

I have taken the afternoon off. Not sure what I am going to do - cinema perhaps?

Love Ed

To: R Henderson
From: Liz
Date: 27/02/08

Dear Bob

Thank you. It is good to have your support. I'm feeling rather helpless at the moment but Grace is a young woman and has to engage with her own recovery. I thought I might invite Dan out for a coffee next week to see how he is. The challenge will be finding a coffee shop which is not staffed by his or Seth's friends! I don't want Grace to feel she is being talked about behind her back, but she has also said she cannot cope with seeing how upset people are about her, and we have to support each other.

Liz

To: Liz
From: R Henderson
Date: 27/02/08

Dear Liz

Thanks for this. I am sure Dan would appreciate it if you can talk to him but you do have more than enough to worry about.

Let me know if there is anything else we can do at
any time.

Bob

It was a huge relief that the SEDS referral had come through. I
liked Martha and felt that she liked Grace and was really worried
about her. I hadn't really thought about trying to help Grace do
less or actively stop her from doing things; although it burned
up calories to drag around a school bag and walk to school she
wanted to do it and otherwise what would she do? Sit in her room
feeling depressed?

SYEDA has a deliberately non-medical policy. They do not weigh
people. They do not ask them how much they are eating. They
talk about the feelings behind the behaviour. Grace had warmed
to this approach and I found that we could talk to each other –
and she could talk about her illness   if we sidestepped the *"What
have you eaten? You can't go on not eating!"* conversations.

Martha's role was different. She had to weigh Grace straight
away. She had to get her to share what she was eating, whether
she was purging, all the hard facts. And she had to tell her the
consequences of that behaviour. At that first meeting she told me
that if Grace continued to lose weight she could be hospitalised in
six weeks or so.

She saw Grace regularly – twice in a week once – and I would sit outside in the waiting room, looking at magazines without seeing them, listening to Magic AM, which plays some great songs "from the sixties, seventies and more". They play it in the MIND shop too. Every now and again when I need sing-along feelgood songs, I will seek it out on the car radio – Magic AM, the choice of mental health professionals.

March

Grace

Things happened so quickly from there. I was seeing Martha on a weekly basis. Martha was lovely, she never said, *"I don't understand"* or *"I don't know what to do"*. She asked me questions, some I hadn't thought about before and sometimes I left feeling slightly hopeful. But the sessions would start off the same – I'd be short with her and would answer questions with a shrug or a one-word answer, and I'd always cry during the session. At times I would divulge something real, a fear I had or something I felt about my family or Dan, but it would take a lot of verbal prodding. Sometimes I'd get so upset I couldn't return from it, I'd sit there and ache with sadness. Not speaking or looking at Martha.

For Rowena's birthday, her mum took three of us to Stratford to see a play. I was anxious, as usual when we got there, and I was really hoping her mum wouldn't make me eat, or ask any questions. As we were getting out of the car, she said she'd treat us to lunch at a pub. The word "Carvery" scared me so much I had a panic attack in the loos. However Rachel managed to calm me down and reassured me we'd just deal with it. I sat with them and did an Arrow-word while they ate.

Martha ordered me about a thousand Fortisip drinks and I kept them in a cool bag at the bottom of my wardrobe. I did try to have one a day, but I'd have to make sure I got up insanely early (5ish) and did loads of walking around during the day.

I was on a half timetable now at school, because I'd dropped Drama and Art, so only had mornings or after-noons. One Friday, I asked to meet Rowena, Rachel, and another friend, Megan, to have a chat. I told them I had anorexia nervosa. I hadn't really spoken to Megan about any of this, but I wanted to share something with her even if it was scary. I felt ready to admit I had an illness. It wasn't just a bad phase. I wanted Megan to know, because I didn't want it to come between us. I had said this a thousand times before, but thought maybe if I told other people it might be more productive.

I went to Dan's afterward and told him exactly the same. I told him how weak I felt – mentally and physically. I could see that he liked being let in, and saw he had hope for me. However on my walk home I felt I had no idea, no tools on how I was going to do "getting better".

In the few weeks leading up to Easter, I barely slept. I'd probably get a couple of hours, get up at about 5 in the morning, and do laundry. I did laundry because I felt guilty for not going to school, and I wanted to help Mum and Dad in any way I could for putting them through the hell of living with me. Even though I knew Anorexia was an illness and I didn't want to have it, I did. And constantly blamed myself. It was my body it was in, and my brain that was going along with its terrible demands. My brain letting the daughter, sister, niece, friend and girlfriend of all of these people destroy herself.

I decided to redecorate my room (I was spending a lot of time in there). I bought a new chair from Oxfam, (for £6!) and started thinking about colours etc. That cheered me up a bit, felt like I had some purpose. I got Dan to help me, but only really so I didn't have to be close with him. I was keeping busy and burning calories, and I could avoid relaxing with him. It sounds awful, but I was repulsed by anything physical. I'd rather avoid being close with him than explain it to him. I hated that he still loved me. I was such a monster – how could he?

I was eating an egg every day – that was it. Sometimes I'd have an orange, or a low-calorie hot chocolate, and then eventually I didn't allow myself the egg. I just had an orange a day. And shitloads of Pepsi Max and Diet Coke.

At one of my meetings, Martha had said I might have to go into hospital, but it just didn't compute in my head.

I was down to about 7 stone. It scared me when she told me, but I'd already given up in my head. I knew the only I way I was going to beat it was to go in to hospital because I didn't feel safe at home any more. I'd started cutting myself and sometimes felt suicidal. I was desperate to go into hospital, but didn't say anything to Mum and Dad, or Martha, because what if they said no? I wasn't ill enough? I was so terrified of my own reactions that I just kept quiet, and did what the anorexia nervosa told me to. *"Just get through the day and earn that orange".*

My next visit to Martha was a Wednesday afternoon. I was wearing a yellow polo neck jumper, jeans and my boots with a heel. I remember looking at my reflection in the window and thinking that my legs looked stupid and I looked so strange, because I was so thin. A little bit of me was still there – it just was really scared. Before my appointment I was sat in the common room with a friend I'd probably not spoken to directly in months. His name was Chris and we'd always got on well, made each other laugh. I told him I was going to a doctor's appointment and he looked worried. He looked at me and wished me luck quietly. I remember thinking that I might never see him again, that I might die, and I felt like he knew that.

I had a huge bag of books and was carrying two folders of work around. Martha commented on how much I was carrying when I came in. We went into the weighing room and I felt really scared suddenly, and started crying. I was suddenly winded; my hands had pins and needles. I felt so panicked and didn't know why. Fear had jumped on my back and panic was rugby tackling me, squeezing me into despair. It was so sudden, Martha looked shocked and she was frowning. I thought that she suspected I was putting it on to avoid being weighed. But I didn't care how much I weighed, I knew I was screwed.

After she weighed me, I calmed down a bit. But Martha looked worried. We went back into the room, and I saw my Dad in the waiting room. (We'd agreed that he should meet Martha and be involved. Before that only my mum had been there and met Martha.) When we were back in the counselling room, she told me I'd lost 3kg in the last week. – I was now down to 6 $\frac{1}{2}$ stone.

She brought my mum and dad in, and said *"I think you'll have to go into hospital, Grace. You've lost nearly half a stone in a week, you're in a very danger—"*

"Good, please, put me in hospital" I cried. *"I'm not strong enough to beat this on my own. I don't care about A levels or Spanish speaking exams, or essays. I just want to*

get better." I cried and begged. I was so relieved to say it out loud. I was just desperate to be in hospital.

Martha made some calls and she organised for me to be admitted the next day. She gave my bag to my Dad and said, *"You're not going to be lugging round all those books any more".* And it did feel like finally I could start sharing the burden, and let people help me.

On the way home, Mum and I went to Matalan to look for some pyjamas, but couldn't find any warm-looking ones. We got some strappy tops, because I wouldn't fit in a bra, and couldn't find any pants that would fit me. We went to Tesco to get shampoo etc. and some oranges. We got home and I had a bath where I ate my orange and drank Pepsi Max.

Later I babysat for a neighbour and she asked me before she left, *"Are you sure you're all right being here tonight?"* I think Mum must have explained things to her. *"Yeah, don't worry about it,"* I said. I felt so relaxed that night, I felt so completely ready for hospital. Not really "relaxed", but the calmest I'd felt in a long time.

When Em got back from school, she came and sat on my chair with me and cried. I told her *"It's gonna be OK. I'm going to get better. It's the best thing for me."* I'd almost forgotten about Emily, because I'd been so wrapped up in my own world. I'd forgotten my best friend.

The next day I sat in my chair with my dressing gown on, and my duvet, and my dad went to town to get me some underwear and PJs. While he was out, I poured my big bottle of Pepsi Max down the drain. I didn't want to need it all the time. I hated it. I felt like it symbolised my weakness.

It was the Thursday before Easter, so Friday and Monday would be Bank Holidays. We left at about 2 in a taxi – me, Mum and Dad. We had all my packed bags and when we got to the hospital we sat in the waiting room for Dr Cipriano to see us. A nurse shouted my name and then weighed me. She seemed really angry and told me off for sitting on the weights wrong. When Dr Cipriano called us in, he asked me loads of questions about how long I'd been ill, why I was unhappy and all that stuff – and it made me want to scream, *"It doesn't matter! All that matters is that I'm here, and I'm in this situation. Please just help me!"*

He said he was thinking about waiting until after the Bank Holiday and I got so angry and started crying and begging not to have to wait until then. Five more days! He decided that we should come back on Tuesday, so I could have a bed on a proper ward and get better care than I would if I went in then, that day. I was gutted. Just so disappointed.

When we got home it was pouring with rain and I fell asleep in my chair. Dad bought me some oranges and fizzy water. Mum and Em went to Matalan and bought me a DVD set with 'You Got Served', 'Honey', and 'Step Up'. We watched 'Step Up' that night. I texted Megan, Lily, Rachel, and Rowena asking them to come over on Saturday and said that it was really important. I thought I may as well use this four days so I could see my friends before I went in, to say goodbye.

Lily, Rachel and Ro arrived together (Megan was in France). We sat in my room and I explained the situation to them:

"I went to see my therapist on Wednesday and I've lost another 3 kilos, I'm really ill. I'm going into hospital on Tuesday - I know it's the best thing for me because I can't do this on my own. It was my decision. I want you all to know how important you are to me and that I love you. I'm gonna get better..."

I started crying, and I could see how worried they were, but they did their best not to show it.

"We're here for you…."

"We'll come and visit whenever we can … you'll be fine."

"I live really close to the Northern General – I can just pop over…"

I could tell they were upset, but they handled it so well.

"Feel free to borrow my clothes", I told them. *"I've got loads and they're really nice. Just pop over whenever you want – someone should be wearing them."* It was the only thing I could think to say to try and make the situation feel a bit more normal.

We started watching the Disney cartoon, Mulan. Me and Rachel were on the bed, Lily in the chair and Rowena by the computer.

"Are you warm enough?" Lily asked me. I was in my dressing gown and had a hot water bottle, and I was still a bit chilly, but I didn't say so.

"Yeah, I'm fine, thanks" I said with a weak smile. I put my head on Rach's shoulder and hugged her. I remember thinking how lovely and warm she felt – firm and comforting. I started crying and whispered to her, *"I don't want to be alone. I'm really scared."*

She hugged me and said softly, *"You're not gonna be alone, hon, you'll be looked after so well and we're all here for you whenever you need us."*

"Thank you. I love you."

"I love you. We all do."

After the film, we all sat on my bed, and just talked about normal stuff. It was really nice but there was the inevitable, underlying feeling of sadness and, for me, fear – as ever.

When they were leaving, they all admired the flowers my mum had bought me and Rach said, *"You'll be getting loads more of them,"* with a smile. After they'd gone I had my orange and did an Arrow word. That night I ordered some audiobooks off the internet, and texted my friend Fran to see what Terry Pratchett I should get. I told her about going into hospital and she sent me a message full of love and concern, as said she'd love to visit me. And to find out if hospitals are like they are on Scrubs. It felt really good to let people know, and to start accepting support.

The next day Mum was taking our little sister Tilly to see 'Horton Hears a Who'. Emily was going too and Mum was really shocked when I asked to come. I thought it would be a nice thing to do before I went in.

When we got to the cinema, we went to the loo and suddenly I felt really scared and sad. I was so overcome by it, and confused. I started crying and Mum asked if I wanted her to take me home. I said no, even though all I wanted was to be in my room, curled up in my chair with a hot water bottle. But I knew Tilly had been looking forward to it, and didn't want to upset her.

I sat through the film, and even managed to enjoy some of it, which was astounding. I was in tears by the end of it, but didn't actually know if they were happy or sad I was so confused.

When we got back I went straight to bed and woke up in the middle of the night. I watched Gok Wan on Catch-Up, and it made me cry. I remember thinking how I wished I could be happy with myself.

The last day before I went into hospital, I asked Dan to come round. I had planned to have a chat with him about us – not the situation with hospital. Because I knew things weren't right with us, and it wasn't just about the anorexia. But my head was such a mess I couldn't work out what was wrong. I knew I didn't fancy him any more, and my feelings had changed towards him – but I didn't know if it was because I disliked myself so much. I resented that he still found me attractive and wanted to love me. Mum asked me how I would feel if he went out with someone else – and I thought I'd be upset, but kind of out of obligation, not love. I wanted to end the relationship then – but I just wasn't thinking straight enough at the time. I didn't want to make any extreme decisions.

I told him that I thought things needed to change and that he should start liking himself more. He looked gutted and really pissed off. Of course he was, it was the most hypocritical advice ever offered. He seemed just as confused as me, actually. He didn't say much, and I got really frustrated because I couldn't really articulate how I felt and what my issues were. We watched one of the many videos he had brought round, but I didn't like it. I feel bad now, for how much I put him through, and that I didn't finish it when my feelings first started changing (around Christmas). If I had just let him go and get on with his life while I wasted mine, I would have saved him the pain of supporting me. I don't blame him for anything that happened, he stuck by me through the hardest time of my life, and I won't forget that.

After he left, Mum and I watched "Oliver!" on my bed. Tilly sat with us while she made a hardboiled-egg fisherman called Eggbert, and Mum knitted him a little hat.

I started to fall asleep and I asked Mum to hold me. She was really shocked – I was asking her to touch me, not just allowing her to. I felt so calm then, I never wanted her to let go.

In the evening my brother Seth came round, and I went and sat next to him on the sofa. He looked at me with a face so full of worry and fear, it made me feel awful. I asked him if he was OK and he said, *"I don't know. I'm scared."* I'd never seen Seth scared before, or at least admitting to it. He was my big brother who was invincible in my eyes. It was so different to how calm and reassuring he was when I first told him I was ill. His concern just made me more determined to get into hospital.

That night, after Seth left, I started to have a panic attack. Mum came and sat on my bed with me. I was so tense, I was digging my nails into the back of my neck and my jaw was like a vice. I was terrified.

Mum said something like, *"I don't know what to do – I can just be here for you."* I told her to just go. I knew she couldn't do anything and she looked so tired. She offered to sleep in my bed but I said no. I didn't want to push her away but I knew she couldn't do anything for me. Only I could help myself. I just didn't know if I wanted to. In the morning I said to her,

"Are you still my friend?" I thought she might have given up on me.

"Yes, I am. But it's just not always very easy to be nice to you." This made part of me angry but I was too tired to get mad. I just accepted it and thought, *"Soon she won't have to babysit me any more."*

I sat in my chair watching TV and Dad came in to say goodbye. He told me not to worry and how brave I was. I didn't feel brave at all. I felt cowardly and small and weak. I asked him if I could get drunk before we went and he smiled and said he didn't think it'd be a good idea. I was getting really scared.

Emily came into my room before she went to school, and sat on my chair with me and cried.

"It's OK hon," I said, *"I'm gonna get better – I know it."* But I didn't know it. I had no idea how long I'd be in hospital for, or if I'd ever get better.

Later on Mum came in and I asked her to buy me some Pepsi Max to help calm me down. I asked her if I could get drunk and she said, *"Well, it might get some calories into you,"* with a smile. Not a happy smile though. It was weak and desperate – exactly how we all felt because of the disgusting thing that had taken over me.

March *Liz*

Texts from this time are a mixture of the everyday and the odd –
a new sort of normality.

Grace to me (27/02/08):
Hey sorry for being short with you this morn. Did you
make any arrangements for those blood tests?

Seth to me (28/02/08):
Hey ma, how big's your wrist? Gonna make you a brace-
let for hallmark Sunday*. Actually do you even wear
bracelets? I can get sth else if you'd prefer it.
Sorry to ruin the surprise x x x

*Mother's Day!

Grace to me (28/02/08):
I have cancelled the massage thing at SYEDA I just
don't feel in the mood

I wasn't surprised by this – the first appointment had made her
feel very uncomfortable. She wasn't letting anyone touch her body.
She would hold my hand but tensed up at any attempt at a hug.

She would tolerate my arm around her but with gritted teeth and a rather desperate *"wish I was somewhere else"* look in her eye. She was constantly cold.

Grace was being intermittently positive at the end of February. Almost every day there would be some time where I felt I could talk to the real Grace, that she would show a bit of spark. She agreed to getting a prescription of Fortisip and tried them in several different flavours, went to Boots on her own for the follow-up collection, got the little fridge down from Em's room to chill them ... but the amount she ate went down and down. I think it was oranges only by this stage. Never eating in front of anyone. Drinking gallons of fizzy water and Pepsi Max. She was supposed to have two Fortisips a day but rarely managed it. I did not nag. I did not insist or even request, that she eat or drink anything against her will.

Her texts to me when I was at work were determinedly upbeat:

Grace to me (04/03/08):
I'll sort the chicken! You look nice today I forgot to say this morning x love you.

Grace to me (05/03/08):
Hi I'm ok thanks. Just went to the coop and got some oranges and I'm gonna do some work now I think. How's work? I love you.

Grace to me (05/03/08):
Yes there's everything in those drinks.

Grace to me (09/03/08):
It's over. I will never own the boots. I am in a glass
cage of emotion and despair. May just have to go to
primark and spend like there's no tomorrow. Rachel
and Ro stood me up as well.I love you x x

It took four appointments for Martha to finish her assessment,
which would lead to a care plan we could implement. The first
was on the 19th of February and the last on the 12th of March.

During this time Grace ate less and less and started looking really
scary, losing the padding from her cheeks, her hands looking
bony and spidery. She scalded her hand filling the ever-present
hot-water bottle and it was streaked red like a port wine stain. I
shudder remembering it, the skinny bony scarred hand.

At the last of the assessment meetings on 12th March Martha told
me that they had discussed the possibility of hospitalisation. She
was still losing weight rapidly and Martha assessed that if her
weight was to go down by another 3kg we would have to look at
Grace being admitted to hospital. In a way this was a relief, to
feel that we did not have to wait for Grace to collapse into a coma,

for her muscles to seize up. I'd read about it, about what happens eventually when your system starts to give up. If the weight loss went past a certain number, Martha would get her admitted. There was no specialist provision in Sheffield, and the closest residential place was in Leeds.

That night Grace went to a classical concert with Dan and I'd agreed to pick her up at the end.

12/3/08 20:20:
Hey is there any chance you could come earlier?

12/3/08 20:20:
Yes, should be OK, why?

12/3/08 20:23:
Don't think I'm gonna make it through the requiem. It's the interval in a bit.

12/3/08 20:24:
I can be there about 8.45 x

12/3/08 20:24:
Sorry you don't have to x x x

She looked awful. Really ill, crumpled up like an old woman. She apologised for dragging me out and I said I didn't mind, but I knew I was feeling angry towards her. I suppose what I meant was, *"It's not THIS that I mind. Don't apologise for asking me to come out and fetch you when you're feeling ill and it's cold and dark. That's fine, it's part of being a parent. If you mind about my feelings and putting us out, for God's sake why can't you choose to start eating and join the human race again?"*

A week later, on 19th March, I met Ed at Martha's clinic for the end of Grace's session. She invited us both in very quickly, then left us with Grace, saying she had to make a phone call. We didn't speak much. A breezy, *"How are you?"* wouldn't have fooled anyone. I squeezed her hand – a standard greeting. We couldn't hug. It felt like hugging a deckchair and you could feel how much she hated it, so that the physical closeness made the emotional distance worse rather than better.

Martha came back and said it had been a difficult session. Grace had reacted badly to being weighed and had lost another three kilos in a week. She had telephoned a consultant endocrinologist who would see Grace the next day. She explained that he would probably arrange emergency admission to a medical ward to address Grace's physical needs. There would be no specialist psychiatric or psychological help available at the hospital. But it was three days before Easter and action had to be taken. Grace's body was not able to take much more starvation.

The weekend passed slowly. Grace was desperate to go into hospital but they postponed it. At the consultant appointment on Thursday she was so scared, begging to be admitted, but the doctor said they could not offer the proper care until Tuesday. I felt helpless and grim, but it was my job to accept the rational explanation and sell that to Grace.

We tried to get her to feel ready, bought new pyjamas, tried to spend some time with her. She has described it well, describing some moments of closeness and some very strained. That time where she asked me to hold her on her bed was special. She allowed herself to be just a little bit soft with me, letting go of the anger and the distance where her despair said, *"It's no good, you'll never understand"*.

Northern General *Grace*

On the Tuesday, Dr Cipriano rang and told me to go in
at about lunchtime to Emergency Admissions. When it
was time to go me, Emily, Mum and Tilly got in a taxi to
the hospital. I was so scared. I had no idea what would
happen when I got there – whether I would have a room
to myself? What kind of people I'd be with? Would they
be nice? Would the make me eat? Or be mad at me if
I didn't? I just didn't know what to expect. But the last
thing I thought would happen is that I would get better,
that I'd be able to eat a meal with my family, or just smile
again.

We arrived at the hospital and met Dad there. We were
told to wait in the A&E waiting room, so we did. Midsomer
Murders was on the big TV on the wall – I think I made a
joke about the quality entertainment. Midsomer Murders
started and finished (two hours) and I still hadn't been
seen by anyone. The nurses weighed me and took my
blood pressure and then told me to go back and wait.
It was awful being sat there. I was freezing so I put my
dressing gown on and tried to lie down because I was so
tired. I just wanted to be at home in my bed. Why would
they tell me to come in if there wasn't a bed for me?

Finally, my name was called and they took me through to the ward. My bed was in the middle of two very old women, and opposite three equally old, distressed-looking patients. I was really confused and didn't know what was going on – I was so tired I just went and lay on the bed. A nice smiley nurse started talking to me and checking my BP; I think she was called Amy. After that, Dad left with Em and Tilly, and Mum sat by my bed while I rested.

The nurses came round with dinner, and I asked for an orange and they brought me two on a plate. A doctor came to see me, but said that she couldn't really do anything to help because it wasn't her area.

Mum had to leave at about 8. I remember I didn't feel extra sad about her leaving – I just wanted her to be able to get on with her life, so I could stop being such a burden. A couple of hours later the nurse came round and turned off all the lights – but I kept mine on and did crosswords, listening to the Stephen Fry podcast. I went to brush my teeth and when I came out the nurse said, *"What were you doing in there? Were you being sick?"*

"No, I was brushing my teeth, honestly!"

"No, I heard you. I know what you were doing. You know you shouldn't do that, it's bad."

"I wasn't! Honestly, I was brushing my teeth!" A part of me wished I was able to throw up – I hated the idea of having food inside me.

Later I asked the nurse if there was somewhere I could go to watch TV; I just wanted to cling on to some shred of normality. She was really helpful and we went to the TV room, but it was broken and wouldn't turn on. I went back to my bed and sat there, listening to the poor old lady next to me mumble, *"Oh dear, oh dear, oh dear."* She never stopped.

At about 2am a male nurse came to my bed and told me I was being moved to another ward – not the right one but a more comfortable one. We got all my stuff together and he offered me a wheelchair, but I said I'd rather walk. We chatted on the way, and I remember being in quite a good mood. I felt like I was getting somewhere.

When we arrived on the ward, I went straight to the TV room and fell asleep there. I woke up at about six and felt horrible. I remember a man (he was bald). He was very jolly and I think he attempted to talk to me but I ignored him and went to my bed and cried. I felt so scared and completely alone. It seemed that my doctor had forgotten I was there. Did I even have a doctor? Did Martha know I was here? I just needed someone to tell me I was going to be OK, but instead, all the nurses were asking me questions.

"Who's your doctor?" *"Should we weigh you?"* I hardly got out of bed that day. I was sat opposite a very old woman, she was very quiet and simply stared. I think I spent quite a lot of time staring back at her, not caring in the slightest if I looked rude. I was miserable and angry for the way I was being treated. The old woman looked so frail, her deeply wrinkled skin seemed to cling to her bones and her eyes bulged out of her face. I'm sure, in fact I've been told, that the picture of us both wasn't that different...

Martha came to see me, and it was so lovely to see some-one I knew, and knew what I was going through. She told me that she was chasing up my situation and talking to the right people. Seth visited me that afternoon and brought me a hot water bottle. I was desperate for one, really cold, but the nurses wouldn't fill it for me because of Health & Safety. Seth and I didn't talk much, I was so angry and sad and nobody seemed to care. After a while I just looked at him and started crying. I held his hand and said, *"I'm so lonely. I just want to go home. Nobody's telling me anything. I'd be better off at home."* In my head I was thinking I'd be better off dead; even the doctors couldn't be bothered with me. Seth made suggestions of things I could do to take my mind off of things like watching TV or listening to music, he was really trying. After he left I watched Midsomer Murders on my little pay-as-you-go bedside TV and managed to fall into a half-conscious sleep that I stayed in for most of the afternoon. Both my parents came to visit in the evening and while they were there, Dr Cipriano finally came in to tell me that I had a bed on the ward where I needed to be. I was relieved, but I didn't trust him, he'd told me this yesterday. He said some nurses would be down soon to take my things and me over, Mum and Dad stayed with me until they did. While I lay there feeling drained and numb, Mum read to me, which I found relaxing and made me less anxious. At about 9 o'clock we were taken over to the new ward, Hadfield 1. I went in the wheelchair, I was too tired to object, and it was quite a trek from where we were.

Hadfield was in the newest part of the hospital, it was a lot brighter than the parts I'd been in, there were loads of windows and you could see out to the real world. I know it had only been 24 hours or so since I'd been there, but it felt like days. I'd lost the energy to be relieved that I was moving to my own room and space; it felt like 'recovery' was slipping through my fingertips.

Over Easter weekend I got in touch with our friends and family and told them about what was going on. I knew it was a hard thing to share – for me to describe and them to hear - but I wanted them all to know. This is an email conversation with my aunt.

From: Liz
Sent: 18 March 2008 13:44
To: janeedgar@waitrose.com
Subject: London

Hi Aunty Jane

How are you? We are OK, but Grace has developed ano-rexia and is very depressed which is tough for all of us. She is getting medical help but recovery is long, slow and not easy (and it doesn't feel like it has started yet.) I am wondering about going to the International Managers' Conference in May (Sounds impressive, doesn't it?) - would you be able to put me up on the 8th? It's a Thursday, and the conference is on the Friday in Hammersmith.

I'm at work so I won't chat, but hope to catch up with you soon,

lots of love, Liz x

From: janeedgar@waitrose.com
To: Liz
Subject: RE: London

Liz

So sorry to hear about Grace. I hope she really is getting the right help.

May 8th/9th is fine for me if you decide to come. It is a bit of a hike to Hammersmith but no doubt you realise that

Love aunty Jane

Hello

Had an appointment with Grace today and she is going to be admitted to hospital tomorrow - so I really don't know how things will be. It is likely to be a long haul and she may have to be in hospital in Leeds for three months - awful, but she is actually desperate for help and cannot do it on her own. To start with she will be in the local hospital just being "stabilised".

Since it has got to this point I'll have to tell lots of people like Dad who don't know she is at all ill. All my sisters saw her in February when we were in North Yorkshire - it was a great week despite G not eating and being obviously very depressed. It's a strange, powerful & scary disease to live with. http://www.b-eat.co.uk/Home has a lot of information. Our local support group is very good, for us as well as her: they lend books and offer support groups which is a lifeline.

I think I may well try to come to the thing in May - but I'll confirm after Easter. Hammersmith may be a trek but it beats trying to catch the 6.05 from Sheffield!

Lots of love
Liz

From: janeedgar@waitrose.com
To: Liz
Subject: RE: London

Dear Liz

I am so upset about Grace and for all of you. Feeling helpless and tearful and I suppose the only con-solation is that it sounds as if il 1s being taken seriously and the right action is being taken.

If I can do anything however unlikely you must let me know. Glad to hear that you have a good local support group and after a quick look at the website I can imagine that would be a lifeline.

Don't know what else to say, but I hope you will feel able to come in May and I have it in my diary

Love to everyone

Aunty Jane

Subject: RE: London
From: Liz
Date: Mon, March 24, 2008 11:03 pm
To: janeedgar@waitrose.com

Hello -

Thank you for your thoughts. The consultant we saw on Thursday actually decided Grace would not benefit by being in hospital over the four-day weekend so she has been at home and will be admitted tomorrow. She has been able to see some friends and her boyfriend, which was good, and we have just watched a lot of films together & got new pyjamas etc. In a way it will be a relief for her to go in, as long as we feel we have faith in the medical staff. She liked and trusted the consultant we saw on Thursday, and he pulled out a lot of stops for her. She got to see a specialist dietician at about 10 minutes' notice, and will get psychiatric help as well once she is admitted. This is a temporary stay on a medical ward while she waits for a place in a specialist inpatient unit - but this may be in Leeds.

All are agreed that she really does want to get better - which is a very positive sign. She is able to talk about how she is feeling and be very articulate about the illness and how scared she is of it, sometimes. I appreciate this - it's much better than when she goes very blank and chilly. I will keep you posted on how things develop -

lots of love,

Liz

Selection of texts from admission day:

25/3/08

Seth:
Hey ma can you keep me up dated with what happens today please. I've got an afternoon off tomorrow and wd like to see grace wherever she's residing x x

Me:

Yeah love I'll let you know. We have been in a&e for nearly 2 hours waiting for a bed. Very fed up and em, tilly & I are starving!

Dan:

hi Liz. Hope everything goes/has gone ok today. I've been asked to play a big gig in London on thurs so wont be here wed + thurs but will be back for Friday. Justin case you want to contact me. Speak soon I hope.

Me:

hey Dan good luck with the gig. We have been here for 4 hours and g has only just got a bed. Everyone else is 90 and it is all a bit depressing. Text me when you're back — and they seem fine about phones so you can text her too. Love Liz.

It must have been 5 o'clock by the time we got a bed for Grace in the Admissions ward. This was an absolute low point. I had dragged myself through the long weekend, another four days after a week of frighteningly rapid weight loss, because of the promise of quality in-patient care. I sat on the hard vinyl benches in the A&E waiting room with Grace lying down, her head on my lap. She stretched out as best she could, her long legs curled awkwardly, wearing her big pale blue dressing gown on top of her clothes. Cold, as ever. Cold, pale, withdrawn, feeling abandoned. Nobody seemed to be expecting us even when we told them the consultant's name. We sat there for nearly four hours, the whole family except Seth, who was working. We had thought we would be able to get Grace settled in and leave her feeling she was *"in the best place"*, *"in good hands"* – all those things you believe about hospitals.

Finally we were shown through to the admissions ward. Even a person who came in quite cheerful would have found it a little depressing. We were not cheerful to start with. There were six beds, three against each wall. Grace was given the middle bed on one side. All the other occupants were very elderly. Next to the window was a lady who moaned with every out-breath. After about an hour she changed this to *"Oh dear"*. Just like that, every painful breath. *"Oh dear (pause) Oh dear (pause) Oh dear"* The lady on the other side kept asking when she was going to go downstairs. *"I've told her it's over there,"* she said to nobody in particular. There were nice nurses who were obviously very busy.

"I'm just going to clean you up, Edna."

"What's that?"

"Going to give you a bit of a clean. DOWN THERE!"

"Oh. Oh all right. What are you doing?"

Doctors came briefly – each person seemed to have a doctor; each doctor who came in saw one patient and showed no interest in the others.

The lady in the opposite corner was quite with it.

"I know what you're going to tell me, doctor."

"What am I going to tell you?"

"You're going to say I've got cancer."

"No, actually, Jean, what I think is happening is that you've got a bit of pneumonia."

Eventually Ed took the other girls home on the bus and I stayed. I couldn't read or anything. Grace dozed. I sat and stroked her hand from time to time or just sat with my hand on her arm.

18.30 from Ed:
hi love how's it going? How's grace?

18:32:
Awful very depressed she is with a doctor now. The ancient people moan and cough and have their nappies changed.

18:35 from Ed:
Yes I know it's crap. It freaked me out. See if they can't move her straight away? Lots of love 2 u both.

26/3/08 08:08 me to G:

Morning darling. I hope you got some sleep with the
moaning oldies. I will ring the hospital a bit later
to see what's happening and come and see you tonight.
Love you loads mum x x

26/3/08 08:20 me to Seth:

hey love grace is still on admissions ward but we
hope she will be moved today. I will ring the hospital late morning and let you know where she is x you
can get various buses including the 88 which I think
comes from Eccy Road.

26/3/08 from Grace:

can you bring me lots of fizzy water please I'm not
gonna get moved til tomorrow. This is a joke. I love
you x x

26/3/08 16:28 me to G:

Hi love will bring loads of water. Did Seth bring a
hot water bottle?

26/3/08 16:30 from Grace:

They won't let me fill it. I'm really low mum I hate
this. I love you x

26/3/08 16.31 me to G:
I love you too hon and wish it could be different x x
x

26/3/08 16.55 from Grace:
Can you bring one of those oranges as well please?
The hospital ones aren't right. They might have a
room for me this evening, fingers crossed x x

"The hospital ones aren't right." That provoked a muffled scream of
frustration from me. This is how anorexia works sometimes, that
crazy rules apply to food and get stricter as the disease progresses.
You can only eat food that is round. Now you can only eat
oranges. That is proper oranges, not satsumas. Maybe they are not
round enough. Now you can only eat navel oranges. The hospital
has common or garden jaffas. As though it made any difference
what you eat, if you are eating so pitifully little – not enough to
keep yourself alive? I did, of course, buy some navel oranges.

26/3/08 22:28 from Seth:
How was yr visit? mine sucked.

26/3/08 22.34 from me:
Fairly awful but they moved her to the proper ward
while we were there which is much better x x x

Got home to good wishes from my sister:

From: Mel
To: Liz

Hi Liz,

Just wanted you to know that we've been thinking of you all today, hope its not been too awful. I didn't want to ring as I suspect you've had enough for 1 day and its important for you to have family time now.

I hope things progress swiftly now and Grace gets the help and support she needs. Know we are thinking of you all and send lots of love and hugs. I'll try and ring towards the end of the week to see how things are going.

I'm here in the meantime should you want a rant about the NHS or such!

Lots and lots of love
Mel xx

Hi Mel

Thanks for your thoughts. It's good to know you are thinking about us, Grace especially. Hideous day yesterday sitting about in A&E for 3 hours waiting for a bed in Admissions, on the ward G surrounded by old people in nappies moaning and coughing or just looking at her at odd angles. No sign of a doctor until 6.15 when the on-call medic came by, etc. etc. Anyway, they moved her to another ward (thoracic/cardiac) at 4 a.m. which was a bit more civilised, but she was very quiet and low all day. It is horrible when she gets so withdrawn. She was seen by a doctor today but wouldn't tell us what he said about the care plan because it was too scary for her(this is part of the reason for the withdrawal). Her therapist from the Eating Disorder service went to see her this morning which I'm pleased about because she will kick some arse! They did finally move her just as visiting time ended this evening - now in a really nice single room with en-suite in the new wing, much more civilised and it brought her out of herself a bit so I felt happier leaving her. Isn't hospital visiting crap?

Lots of love
Liz

Subject: Grace
From: Liz
Date: Fri, March 28, 2008 9:35 pm
To: Many

Dear All

Thank you for all your thoughts and prayers over the last week.

Grace is now settled in the proper ward she is supposed to be in, in the newest wing of the hospital with a big single room and private bathroom (but right opposite the nurses' station and they pop in and say hello on a regular basis).

She has seen the consultant endocrinologist, consultant & registrar psychiatrist, and dietician yesterday, and they decided to start tube-feeding straight away. I saw her with the tube in yesterday - not as bad as I had feared and she was much happier than Wednesday. They will continue with tube-feeding until she is "stabilised" but I don't know what that means, whether it is a specific weight or some other measure. Then they will start giving her anti-depressants and some CBT while continuing the tube feeding before moving on to eating. It is very hard to understand but she is really scared by the idea of eating.

Her therapist from the Sheffield Eating Disorders Service, who made sure she got admitted in the first place, went to visit her yesterday and then again today. She is lovely and very mild-mannered but has been kicking some serious behind to get Grace seen by the right people and some action taken quickly. Grace has also been making friends with the regular nurses on her ward now she is settled (and the cleaner, Mohammed).

If you want to send her anything, she now has a portable DVD/CD player and would like audio books. Email/text if you want suggestions for DVDs since she has many donations already. It's nice to have cards etc. sent to the hospital as well since they arrive at a different time from visitors.

Lots of love to you all -

Liz

Hadfield 1 *Grace*

The ward was quiet, with some nurses pottering about seeing to various patients. It was a mixture of private rooms and sets of beds with curtains around them like the ones I'd been in before. My room was... well it was that. A room. It had a bed, a chair, a bathroom and a window. We went in and I sat on the bed, awkwardly said goodbye to my parents, waving at them from a few feet away and I was left alone. I didn't feel ready to attempt sleep yet, so I went to the big TV room and watched 'Desperate Housewives' in a big chair. I felt comfortable, and finally ready to settle somewhere, trying not to think about what tomorrow would bring, I made my way back to my room and really appreciated my new fresh surroundings.

One of the main things I cherish about my time in hospital, are the people I met. On the first day it was Tim. He came in and chatted to me. He asked me about my anorexia:

"What do you eat? How did you get like this? You're so young..."

111

I remember speaking to the dietician that day and she explained that I needed to start getting some nutrition in me and to start a food plan.

"What do you mean? What kind of food?" I panicked. The very mention of actual food made my head spin.

"I don't know, maybe a piece of toast for breakfast, a sandwich at lunch..."

"No, I really don't think I'd be able to do that. I'm not ready for that."

I thought to myself, *"What am I ready for then? Will I ever be strong enough to eat?"*

"OK," she said. *"That's fine. We can take things slow. There's also the Fortisip supplement drinks – "*

"They're disgusting!"

"Yes, I know they're not ideal, or to everyone's taste. If you could try with them though..."

"I don't know."

"Well, we could give you the tube feed. You'd have to have a tube going in your nose, which goes down to your stomach. That would be attached to a supplement and we could put it on at night. It needs 12 hours for it all to go in."

"OK, OK, let's do that!"

The thought of having to put a tube down my throat didn't faze me at all – I was so detached from my own pain I didn't even think about the tube going in. It would be there feeding me, which was more than I could do for myself.

"Great", she said. *"Well, we can start that tonight – it'll be a relatively small dosage because we don't want to over-load your system. I'll get a nurse to put the tube in this afternoon, and the feed will start about 10, and finish at 8 tomorrow morning."*

"Right."

"Excellent. OK, Grace, I'll be in to see you in a few days. If you have any questions or anything just let one of the nurses know, because I'll probably be around."

She gave me a gentle smile, which I found encourag-ing. She was so understanding and straightforward. She didn't get frustrated when I refused the food, the Fortisips. She just accepted it and carried on. I really felt that she appreciated how hard it was for me just to be there – to accept help.

Seth came in that afternoon about 2. He said I looked happier to be there than the day before. I was surprised to see him.

"Haven't you got work today?"

"No, I'm not going in this week."

I wondered why for a minute and then it struck me that it might be because of me. I hadn't thought about how this might be affecting him. As he didn't live in our house any-more I assumed he was more detached than my parents but that wasn't true at all. I wondered if they talked about me at home? I just thought they would carry on, now that I was out of their way in hospital. I never thought it would stop them doing anything. No, it must be some-thing else, I thought.

A bald man in a white shirt came in to take some blood while Seth was there. He was very jolly and friendly.

"Hiya sweetheart, how are you?"

"I'm all right thanks."

"Good stuff. I'm sorry to interrupt. I couldn't get in earlier; I think you were with your doctor. Anyway, I won't be long."

"It's fine," I said lazily.

He gave Seth a nod and started getting on with cleaning my arm and getting the needle ready.

"Whereabouts d'you live then?"

"Meersbrook. Do you know it? Not many people do."

"Oh aye, near Heeley?"

"Yeah."

"Yeah, I know Meersbrook. Nice area. You know Meersbrook's the only parish in Sheffield that doesn't have a pub?"

"Really? What about the Red Lion on Chesterfield Road?"

"That's technically in Heeley," he nodded.

"No, that's not right," Seth piped up. *"Meersbrook's not the only one. Greystones doesn't have any pubs either."*

"It does mate, what about The Banner?"

"That's in Banner Cross" Seth replied, sounding a bit peeved at having his pub knowledge challenged.

"Nah, Greystones, mate. It's only Meersbrook that doesn't have one single pub."

I could see Seth holding back. He was really itching to argue. I could see him going on Wikipedia in his mind, finding some way to prove him wrong.

I thought I'd break the atmosphere. The blood-taking was not going well.

"Sorry, I've got pretty stingy veins. Do you want to try the other arm?"

"Yes, sorry, love. Let's have a go on the other side." He smiled at me and had a go at my left arm. After a few attempts he eventually got enough and gathered up his things.

After Seth left, two psychiatrists came in to talk to me – an Asian man who looked about in his late 20s and a woman in her late 30s. The both looked very professional, but not intimidating with it. Sometimes people can look too smart, I think.

I can't remember what they said to me, to get me to open up, but somehow we got talking. I was crying.

"I just feel hopeless. I don't feel like I deserve food ... I don't deserve anything. I've put my family through so much I'm just not worth it."

"Worth what, Grace?" the woman asked gently.

I was silent for a few minutes. I just sat and thought about my answer. I genuinely couldn't think of any reason for me to be alive.

Eventually I sighed out one word.

"Life."

There was a long pause while I cried. I think they were waiting for me to elaborate, but I was done.

After a while, the woman spoke.

"Well, you're clearly in a very bad place and the most important thing to us is your mental state. As you're so young, we have to be careful what kind of medication we prescribe. There is an option of one which would increase your appetite ... would you consider that?"

Immediately I replied,

"No! Please no."

I thought to myself, the last thing I want right now is to be hungrier.

"OK. Well, we'd advise a very small dose of Prozac. It'll be in syrup form as a tablet would be too much for your body."

"OK."

"Then hopefully once your mood improves, we can start to think about some other therapies to improve your body image and self esteem. There is a method called CBT which is Cognitive Behaviour Therapy, looking at how you see yourself and improving confidence, self-esteem."

I started to perk up then. I remember thinking about the future right then, and not being scared. For a moment I thought I could change. I thanked them, and they said they'd be in touch soon about the medication.

At about 4pm Tim and another nurse came in to put my tube in. It was a sunny afternoon. I remember there being a lot of light in the room. I was sitting in the chair by my bed, and Tim started to put the tube in. It went up my nose and then down the back of my throat – well, it was meant to. It got stuck on the bend and I could feel it cutting into the flesh. Tears stung my eyes and I thought to myself, *"I'm not going through this again. However much I don't want to eat, nothing is worth this pain."*

"I'm really sorry, sweetheart," said Tim. *"I'll try again. Have some water, it's probably because your throat's dry. I'm really sorry. I promise it'll work this time."*

He tried to soothe me, smiling sympathetically.

"OK", I said in a weak crackly voice through a face full of tears. *"It really hurts."*

"I know, love, but it's got to be done."

He could clearly see how upset I was and I felt he was doing everything he could to make this as easy as possible. In my mind I felt no anger towards him, which shocked me, because that was usually how I felt about people who tried to help me. But I was so thankful to him then, not that I would show it. I was too scared that anorexia would catch me and attack. It was easier to stay sullen and safe from it.

The tube finally went down and my throat felt like it was on fire, but my head felt calm. I think I was too tired to be angry or upset. I was making my first steps to actually getting better. Not talking about it, or thinking about how hard it was – just doing it.

Emily and Mum came to see me that night, with bags of goodies! They'd brought me a portable DVD player – which I felt really guilty about. It looked expensive as anything. There were cans of Pepsi Max, bottles of fizzy water, and best of all, Emily brought photos from our last summer holiday. A few from Spain and a couple from camping in Wales – ones of us and Tilly. They meant so much to me. We looked so happy in them. They reminded me of who I was, before anorexia kidnapped me. The girl I missed, who had space in her brain to love and laugh and enough flesh on her bones to fill a bikini.

I didn't take in how different I looked in them, to how I looked right then. Emily said she was thinking about dyeing her hair dark brown, and she'd bought some Ugg boots off the Internet. These sorts of things just had no meaning. They had become alien to me and I just accepted it like there was nothing I could do to change this. However much I wanted it to, I just didn't think I was strong enough. I watched "A Cinderella Story" that night after they'd left, and cried at the ending. It wasn't necessarily sad tears, exhausted, yes, but not entirely sad.

When I woke up the next morning I felt restless and anxious straight away, probably because I'd been asleep but also it was my first night with the feed – I wanted to get up and move, and not be taking in the horrible pale sick-coloured feed they had me wired up to. I sat out of bed in my chair. The ward was really busy. I saw Hazel run past my room lots, as other nurses went around offering breakfast to everyone. There was the painfully appetising smell of sausages in the air, which actually drove me to tears. I could feel myself getting more and more angry and anxious as the time went by. My chest felt tight, like someone was wringing my lungs. Still no-one came.

"They said it would stop at eight – that's what I agreed to, and now they're just taking the mick," I thought. *"They tricked me. They lied."*

The blood test guy came in again and tried to chat with me, but I just sat there and cried. He could see I wasn't in a good place and smiled warmly, but sadly. He said,

"Not feeling quite right today? That's OK."

He got the blood and went on his way.

After what felt like forever, Hazel came in and got rid of the feed. I was really angry by then. I couldn't even speak I was so disappointed in myself. Anorexia was really punishing me for accepting the feed.

That morning I was really drowning. "Grace" was a very long way away – tied up, gagged, and she had given up. Her eyes were slowly closing and all the muscles in her body were being slowly wrung out by the ugliness.

I lay in my bed and wept silently. I was too tired for anger. I was utterly self-involved – All I could do was think about how much I hated and resented my own existence. There was nothing else.

Martha came in at about 11, and sat by my bed.

"Hi, Grace, how are you?" she said, in her usual soft, friendly voice.

"I'm really bad. I'm..." I couldn't find the words, and tears took over yet again.

"Hmm. You're not in a good place today, are you?" She sounded concerned – but like she understood, and that meant a lot to me.

"No, not at all."

There was a pause. I think she could see I was trying to get something across. The pause went on.

"What's upsetting you today, Grace?" she asked.

"I feel weak. I feel like I've failed. I'm a failure. I'm an idiot ... I'm so stupid." I relayed everything the voices in my head were muttering and spitting at me.

"Why do you feel like this, Grace?"

"Because it's true. Because I've given up, by getting this." I gestured to the tube in my nose.

"Don't you think that makes you stronger? Don't you want to get better? That's why you're here, Grace." She spoke

slowly and carefully; very aware that anything she said could provoke those voices to really hurt me – to take over.

"I'm here because I'm weak, and I'm not strong enough." Then the voices said what I was dying to...

"Give up, Grace..."

So I did, right then. I just cried. I turned my head away from Martha.

"Are you having any visitors today, Grace?"

Long pause.

"I hear your Mum was in last night."

Really long pause.

"That's a nice painting, isn't it?" She pointed to the land-scape painting on the wall facing us. *"Do you know where that is?"*

I had gone far beyond small talk about paintings.

"No, you're not here today, are you?" said Martha. *"OK then, Grace, I've got to go. I'll let Hazel know when I'll be in next. All right?"*

"OK. See you soon."

I don't remember what I did after she left. I probably didn't get out of bed. It's odd to think about how little I felt capable of. I had such a lack of drive or passion for anything other than not eating. When I was at home, I'd put it all into walking, laundry, anything to keep busy, keep burning energy I told myself I didn't deserve. In reality I didn't have any energy: where that drive came from was pure will, and a really deep sadness.

That Friday, 2pm came, and so did Seth, as usual. He was a rock throughout it all, understanding – and even if he didn't, just accepting and never giving up. He sat by my bed and asked me how I was. I told him I wasn't feeling very good. Conversation must have been quite ropey because we resorted to doing a crossword. Have I talked about the crosswords yet? Doing them (and laundry, bizarrely) was how I passed the time. Arrowords were my favourite, they were really easy on my starved brain. I'm not sure what it was in particular about them – maybe it was that they didn't ask anything of you and I could ask people for help – I think I would have completely lost touch with Chris if it hadn't been for Arrowords in the common room.

Anyway, we were doing a crossword from one of my extensive collection. We didn't finish it, because the female psychiatrist came in for a chat. She asked if I wanted Seth to stay or not, and I decided I'd be more honest if he wasn't there. He stood up, and Hazel showed him to the TV room where he could wait.

I was still feeling anxious – my stomach was tense and my legs felt a bit furry. It wasn't very noticeable, just lingering there.

As we talked, the lady asked me questions gently and slowly. She asked me about how I'd been, how Seth was, then about the feeding tube. That was when things got scary.

I started to cry, and then my stomach knotted up so tight I thought my body might twist right off my legs. I was used to the tummy twists though; what really scared me was my legs were tingling – more than tingling, they were fizzing. They didn't feel like part of me any more.

I was scared then, really scared, because I felt so lost and under attack. The more I thought about it and let the voices in my head spit vicious words at me, the more angry I would get. I stood up out of bed, and threw a bottle across the room at the wall. I blamed my anxiety on some lemonade I had drunk earlier.

"I'm such an idiot!"

"Worse than that, mate..." said the voices.

"I'm so stupid!"

"You got that right. Why are you here?"

"I wish I wasn't here!"

"What do you mean by that, Grace?" The psychiatrist asked quietly. She had stayed sitting down, as I paced the room and hit the walls.

"I wish I was dead. I don't know why I'm here. I'm a waste of space. I'm shit. I'm just weak, and useless, and I shouldn't be here!" I half-screamed, through a clenched jaw and gritted teeth.

I was so angry, every inch of feeling I had was pure hatred and disgust at my own existence – there was nothing else. I went over to the window and hit it with the heel of my hand. I considered opening it, to try and get out – there was a pathway outside into another building – but I knew someone would stop me, and even in that rage, I knew I didn't have the physical strength to do it. This thought fuelled me again. I carried on crying, screaming into my jaw.

The psychiatrist had stood up when I was by the window. Now she tried to get me to sit down.

"Why don't you sit down, or get into bed? It might help you to relax."

"No, I can't. It – It's just – it – it's too -" I couldn't explain the agony my brain was in. All of my muscles felt tight, and contorted, and I felt there was nothing I could do to control it. The anger was starting to subside now, and I just wanted to be able to calm down. The voices had worn themselves out and Grace was trying to take hold.

"Have you tried any relaxation techniques to help you when this happens?" asked the lady, quietly.

"No, no I haven't. Maybe I should. Yes, Yeah, maybe that'd help," I stuttered. I was still crying, but was just desperately trying to cling on to my own voice in my head, terrified of the other voices attacking again. Then I lowered myself into my bed, trying to calm my breathing.

"OK," she said, *"let's give it a go now then. I'll just talk you through it, and you can try it whenever you want to."*

I lay in my bed, still terrified and rigid. She softly explained that I should go from the very bottom of my body, tensing and then releasing every muscle, concentrating on nothing but my breathing. It did really help, and eventually I did manage to feel quite rested. Once I was settled she got up to leave, and asked if I wanted my brother to come back in. I didn't open my eyes I was so scared of getting angry again.

"No. I just want to stay like this. I just want to relax", I whispered, thinking the voice might not hear me and disturb my rest. I wanted Seth to leave anyway. I hated the idea of him making time and effort to come and see me – he should be doing something worthwhile with his time.

Dad came to see me that night. I was still feeling really anxious and uneasy, and after about an hour, I started getting pins and needles in my feet and legs. *"Not again,"* I thought. *"Please, just leave me alone"*. My chest started fluttering. It felt like there was an angry rabbit stuck there, thumping its feet.

"I don't feel right. Hmmm –" that noise was quite high-pitched, more of a moan. I stood up and started pacing by my bed. Dad looked really confused and worried. He asked if I wanted a doctor, and I remembered the female psychiatrist saying there was always someone like her on call if I needed them, so I asked Hazel if she could get someone to come and talk to me. I didn't even know what was technically happening: I think it was a panic attack. I hadn't had my orange yet that day, and thought it might have been that. As I was pacing in my room with

Dad, I started crying. I felt so lost. Dad stayed sitting down, and tried his best to comfort me. Thinking about it, the natural thing to do in that kind of situation would be to go and hug him – let him comfort me; but my illness had broken that instinct. It made me hate to be touched and to despise any kind of sympathy. It was my fault I was upset, so why should anyone feel sorry for me?

"Why don't you try and sit down, love?" Dad asked from his seat.

"No, no..." I moaned. *"Why can't I do this? No..."*

The voices in my head were telling me to give up, that I was worthless and weak, to give up.

"No! I'm here to get better," I cried, my head in my hands. *"It's OK".*

I tried to control my breath, breathing out slowly. I got back into bed. I told Dad I was going to try and do what they psychiatrist had taught me. As I started to relax my chest calmed down. I still had pins and needles in my legs, but I was regaining a bit of calm.

I sat up and talked to Dad, trying to explain – but I just wanted to forget. I started watching the Family Guy DVD Seth had brought me, and I held Dad's hand as I watched.

I turned to him and said,

"I'm so glad you're here."

I was really clinging on to my slightly relaxed mood, terrified of switching again. I laughed out loud at the DVD – I don't know if it was genuine, or I was over-compensating and trying to convince myself I was OK. Either way, it worked. It came to 8 o'clock and Dad left. Then I had my orange. About an hour later, a psych I hadn't met yet came into my room, and we talked for a bit but I can't recall it being of any great importance. I couldn't understand the mental battle, and it was wearing me down.

The next morning was Saturday. I remember it being really bright and sunny – there were lots of windows on the ward, so the weather always changed how it felt inside. Hazel was my nurse for that day, which made me happy. She just seemed to know what to do and was always so calm about everything. Matter-of-fact, that's what she was. The breakfast trolley came round and offered me some – it was the small nurse in dark blue. She had the same reddy-coloured hair as Debbie the tea-lady but it was a bit longer. When I said, *"No, thank you"* she gave me a bit of a dirty look, and sighed.

Hazel was in my room, sorting out my feed tube, and I said to her,

"Hazel, I feel really bad saying no to her. I don't think she likes me. She looked right annoyed at me."

"Don't worry," she said, *"It doesn't take much for her to look like that."*

This was another time when I was reminded of the rest of the world going on, whether I noticed it or not. I found I was interested, I wanted the hospital goss.

"Ooh, is she not very nice? Or just mardy?" I asked, intrigued.

"Hmm." Hazel wasn't giving anything away. I decided I would be wary of that nurse from then on, if she was mardy. Hazel started to leave and I said,

"Hazel?"

"Yes, love?" She turned back towards me.

"I am trying. I'm trying really hard."

"I know. Just do what you can. You are here to get better." She said it in a tone that made me feel like I could do

better, but not in a bad way. It was more encouraging. It felt a bit like she understood.

Then I wrote, on the first page of my new blank diary Rach had given me for Christmas:

FUCK OFF ANOREXIA!

It felt like I was taking a huge risk. It gave me such a rush of empowerment, like I was slapping away anorexia's cold hard gripping hand from round my neck. I was so thrilled I rang home, to tell Mum and Dad. Mum sounded happy to hear from me, and I was relieved to hear her sounding happy. I imagined them in the house, with the front door open doing Saturday morning things. Filling the house with light and fresh air, in their new breathing space. For the first time in a while I missed it.

I got out of bed that day, and one of the community workers, Sarah, made my bed. I felt really spoilt. I made an effort to stay out of bed that day; I sorted things out in my room, and did some Arrowords, and Mum came to see me with Tilly during the afternoon. I can't recall anything else from that day – I guess Dad came in the evening.

Lily had texted me and we'd arranged for her to come and visit me on Sunday afternoon. I wanted so much to make her happy to see me and see how hard I was trying. I wasn't sure how I should be with her, whether to avoid talking about it or not.

Sunday morning came around – it was strange because I was actually woken by the nurses. This meant I had been asleep, which was very surreal for me at the time. Sleeping was something the illness made me feel was a luxury I didn't deserve. So knowing that I had been asleep made me feel very anxious from the second I was woken. My nurses were also two people I had never met before, which made me feel more uneasy, but I had to suppress it. One of the nurses was a tall man with dark hair, and the other was a shorter, curvy Indian woman with long dark hair tied back into a bun. She got out all of my various pills I took, and made sure I squirted the mini-syringe of Prozac into my mouth. The pills tasted disgusting.

"Come on, they help you get stronger, help make you better," she prompted.

"I know, I know," I said, knocking them back. I noticed her name badge said *"Nina"*. She asked me if I wanted breakfast, as the trolley came wheeling round. Luckily the people wheeling the trolley were people I recognised. It was really confusing me not being around familiar faces. I felt like I'd woken up in the wrong place, and this

woman was speaking to me like no one had in a very long time. She was like a busy mum, treating me like the child I was. When I said no to the breakfast, she gave me a questioning look. I wondered if maybe she didn't know I had anorexia.

"I've had that all night," I said, gesturing to the feed.

"Yes, but you need to eat – you are very skinny. You need to get bigger. Have something?"

"No, I'm sorry."

"You must have something!" This took me by complete surprise. No one had spoken to me like that in a very long time – out of fear, I suppose. It was quite nice, in a strange way, to be treated like a normal person.

"Everyone must eat!"

"I'll have an orange," I blurted out, not even thinking. I just wanted her to stop hassling me. So I said that, and I felt so brave. A million things were going through my mind then:

"If you have it now, what will you do for the rest of the day? Will you have tea, or coffee?"

I ignored them, listened to the nurse, and ate the orange.

I was absolutely terrified: this was a morning completely out of my routine. Strangers, strangers who tried to get me to eat, like they would anyone else, and now I was eating an orange in the morning, without having thought about it for days or "earning" it. Just doing it. Just to please the sweet, pushy nurse I'd known for five minutes. I felt like I was standing in the middle of a busy road full of angry drivers, just waiting for one to mow me down. I finished the orange. So elated with myself I was, that when Sarah popped her head round the door to see if I was OK and say hello, I asked her for some orange juice!

"You're really pushing it now," the voices warned.

"Shut up, shut up!" I blocked them out, but I could hear and feel my heart fluttering.

Sarah came back with the juice, and I drank it. There was a lot going on in the ward, all the nurses and community workers were running to and fro past my room. I got up to open the curtains and then got back into bed. My mood was quickly going down. I hated myself for eating that orange. It just created so much disgust, I couldn't think of anything else. I sat in bed and cried. I was surrounded by awful thoughts.

"What's the point? Why are you even here? Give up. You don't deserve to be here. Idiot. You don't make anyone happy, just a waste of space, that's what you are."

I could see, hear, feel nothing but how much I despised myself then. This feeling swelled and took over my body then, every muscle and down to the bone. I cried so hard that I started to scream.

As I was doing this, a short woman with spikey hair was trying to clean my room – I made no effort to hide how I was feeling for her sake – it wouldn't let me. I didn't see the point.

"Are you all right, love? Do you want me to get someone?"

I couldn't speak. I was up on my knees on the bed now; I kept hitting my thigh, digging my knuckles in as I attacked myself. The cleaner left and came back to say that a nurse was coming as soon as possible. I didn't see what good that would do. I was completely out of control at that point. The part of me that would have been trying to use the relaxation techniques was so far from any power in my mind, I was utterly consumed by depression.

"The nurses don't even care about you, and they're paid to! You may as well give up. Just end this pathetic act that you want to recover. Give up. Just give up."

The cleaner, poor lady, had no idea what to do. She tried to busy herself with my room, but was probably scared to leave me alone to wait for the nurse. I got out of bed and started pacing the room, hitting the wall and my thigh alternately. I was now thinking of ways I could actually kill myself.

I had only ever cut my thighs with nail scissors, thought about taking a few packets of paracetamol, but I'd never yearned for it like this.

"It's the only way I'll be free from this. So will everyone else."

When I'd thought like this before, the thought of my Mum and Dad always stopped me. The last thing I wanted to do was upset them, but right then I honestly thought they were better off without me. The best thing I could do for them was die. At least the memory of me would be silent, still. Not the monster called Grace that had started prowling the house.

The window. I thought if I could get out of the window I could just run in front of a car and that would be it. Over. Easy.

As I was crawling back on to my bed with my head on the mattress, I dug my nails into the back of my neck as hard as I could.

Nina came into the room. The cleaner had gone by now. She pulled curtains over my door. I stood up so that the bed was between us. She came over to me and I turned away. She tried to calm me down.

"What's wrong? Come on now, why don't you sit down?"

"No, No..." I cried. She was a lot shorter than me – her head was about the height of my chest. I was wondering if she would stop me if I did make a break for the window. Would I actually get through? I went to the window and opened it as wide as it would go. Nina stood in front of me and put her hands gently on my elbows and tried to calm me. I carried on crying and walked to the other side of the room, but not as fast as I had before. I was beginning to just feel weak – in every sense. I felt too weak to maintain my hunger, but not strong enough to fight the demon in my head. I saw no way out. Dying was literally my best option, in my mind.

Nina followed me again and this time she sat on the bed and said,

"Will you come and sit with me? I want to talk to you about something. Will you come and listen to me?"

"I don't want to sit down. I just wa-"

"Come on, just sit. It will help you calm down."

She held my elbow very gently again. And out of pure politeness I sat down. Suddenly it cracked - I thought, I've been rude enough, come on Grace, give her a chance. I don't know where these sensible thoughts came from, but they managed to fight through the ugliness and reach me.

I sat down next to her, still crying.

"That's it," she said. *"Now, have you ever heard of Jesus?"*

"Oh no, here we go," I thought. *"She's gonna tell me that God loves me so every thing's fine and dandy."*

Out loud, I said, *"Yeah, I don't really believe in any of that."*

Nina wasn't fazed. She went on,

"Well, I do, and can I show you something?"

"Yeah."

She reached into the pocket of her trousers and got out her purse. Out of it she pulled a picture of a round-faced, smiling little boy.

"This is my son, his name is Sammy."

"He's beautiful." – and he really was. His eyes were bright and happy.

"Yes he is. But he can't talk. He understands but he has no words. He's never said a word in his life and he is nine."

"Why?"

"We don't know." She shrugged.

Listening to Nina really brought me out of myself, hearing about someone else, completely detached from my life and me. She continued:

"We've seen doctors, therapists, and still nothing. And I ask God – why? Why have you done this to my boy? I don't know. And it makes me sad of course; I can't speak to my son. But you know what?"

I assumed she was going to say that she gets on with life and everyone's got issues and I should stop feeling sorry for myself.

"He is gifted, so gifted. He is a very musical little boy, always on the piano tinkling away. You sing a tune and he can play it." She smiled. And so did I.

Nina went on: *"I could sit and cry about how awful it is that my darling boy can't speak a word, but where would that get me? I know God has blessed my boy."*

She stroked the picture and I thought how strong she must be. I thought,

"That's great that she can see the brighter side, and her son's gift. I still don't believe in God. I'm still weak. If there is a God, he'll have definitely given up on me."

"You must be very strong," I said – with envy, I suppose. Nina shrugged.

"I have my faith. Now will you pray with me?"

I was a little shocked, but agreed. Nina stood up. I stayed sitting down and she put her arm around me. I leant my head on her as she prayed. After she'd done, we both said *"Amen."*

"Right. Are you going to have a shower today then?"

"Um. OK." Hygiene was one of the things that had taken a sideline in my life, and I hadn't washed since I'd come into hospital. I think I changed my pyjamas and maybe wiped myself with a baby wipe, but that was it. I was always too cold to shower at home, so I had baths – but they didn't have any baths in hospital.

"Right, well, where are your wash things?"

"Um, my shampoo and conditioner are in there." I gestured to the bathroom door leading off form my room.

"Do you have a hair brush? Soap?" she asked

"No."

"OK, Well, I'll find you some. Do you have clean clothes to put on? Pants and a bra?"

"I've got clean pants." I'd given up trying to wear a real bra. I still had boobs, surprisingly, but nothing worthy of a bra. Mum had brought me a crop top with support in though, to keep me warm at least.

"And I've got tops, but no clean trousers."

"Well, I'll find you some pyjama bottoms then. You wait here and I'll get your things."

I felt strange: the lack of routine had really taken me by surprise. I was very wary of new things, and I'd got used to strictly planning everything – what I'd allow myself to do, eat, watch, and what my limit would be. Now I'd never been in this situation and didn't know what to expect. I know I was safe. I was still in shock from how Nina had managed to calm me down, and I felt numb. I was in so much pain I just didn't know how to express it, short of cutting myself. When she came back, she closed the curtain over the door and we both went into my bathroom. She was carrying a towel, a comb, some soap and some huge blue and white hospital pyjama bottoms.

She helped me out of my own pyjamas. They smelt lived-in, and I was relieved to get them off. As I took my pants off I saw the stains in them – the results of my laxative-abused bowels – I remember I wasn't even embarrassed, and Nina didn't bat an eyelid.

Once I was undressed, Nina swung out the shower-chair and helped me sit in it, and then she gently swung me back. All the time she was calmly chatting to me about nothing in particular, which was very soothing for some reason. I felt so looked-after.

As she washed me, I didn't feel scared or uneasy at all. My chest wasn't pounding, and I didn't feel uncomfortable about being naked in front of this stranger. Just accepted, cared for and calm. The water was warm and gently massaged my skin. Nina rubbed my back with the soap and then handed it to me to do the rest of my body.

As I let Nina wash me, I thought about how long it had been since I had let anyone touch me, care for me. I had spent the last six months pushing people away and punishing myself, but this felt so natural, to just sit and enjoy the hot shower. The water felt like every hug I'd pushed away from my mum and dad, every touch I'd avoided – just raining down on me, with all of Nina's warmth. I closed my eyes and let these emotions run through my body. It sounds like such a cliché, but that's exactly how it felt – a wash, tingling the inside of every part of me. My head, chest, fingers and legs – all just relaxing, being looked after: why had I forgotten how this felt?

Thinking about it now, I probably hadn't sat down in months without feeling guilty. Most of the time, I felt guilty for existing, let alone the luxury of a hot shower. It felt like a weight had been lifted, not a huge one, but something about the simplicity of life and the way you live, your own impact on the world, started to make sense.

"That was lovely," I said quietly, as Nina helped me out of the shower.

"Thank you." I didn't smile, or even look at her, but I felt so incapable of showing any kind of happiness or gratitude for support. Something anorexia had me scared of – I felt as though if I smiled, or laughed, it would catch me, like a teacher coming in the room as you are writing naughty things on the board. Nina shrugged and said,

"Everyone deserves a shower. You should wash every day." I couldn't really argue with that.

Then she helped me get dressed; again exclaiming about how skinny I was (which I shrugged off). She found one of my crop top things and said,

"This is very pretty, you should wear this."

I knew I'd be freezing in it, and part of me was thinking, *"Why should you want to look pretty? You're disgusting."* But the larger part of me was reminded of my grandma by Nina – and I would never say no to my grandma. So I put the top on, and wasn't too cold.

I felt a bit embarrassed then, because I'd been in such a state before, and felt that maybe she thought I was a brat or just loopy. I still didn't quite understand why she was being so nice to me.

Nina left after that. After all, she did have a ward to look after.

My mood got worse when she had left. I remember just being bored, and I think that's how it started getting worse – having nothing to do but think about where I was and why. I sat down to watch some Family Guy, in hope it would put me in a better mood. A new psychologist (a young man with short blond hair this time) came in to see me while I was watching it. He asked me what had triggered my attack earlier, and I said it was because I had an orange and some juice. He suggested that maybe I don't eat if it's going to get me in such a bad state mentally. This really threw me.

"What? What do you mean? That I shouldn't even try?"

"Well, as you do have the tube feed, it's not compulsory if it upsets you that much to eat."

"So I shouldn't eat at all? But I like having my orange..." I started crying. I felt like he was taking away my only allowance. He sighed, and looked annoyed at me, but he was probably just looking for the right thing to say.

"No, I'm just saying your mental state is of the utmost importance here. We just want to keep you safe. So don't do anything that will endanger you. If you want to eat, and feel that you can, go for it – but don't push it for other people's sake."

Other people's sake was the reason I was there. I didn't know what was going on, I didn't know whether I would eat another orange later on as usual, or try and kill myself, or rip out the nose tube.

I sat and cried for a while, and then I remember just wandering around my room. Battling in my head what to do, I picked up my diary that I'd scribbled little things in over the past few days, and I ripped out all of the pages with something on. Maybe if I'd read my message to anorexia it could have helped, but it didn't. I was so angry. Just purely angry – nothing else.

I hit myself then, with the diary, on my head, my legs. I really wanted to hurt myself. I looked in the medicine bowl with the bits for my tube in, to see if there were any scissors in there, but there weren't, thank God.

Now I was even angrier, that I couldn't cut myself. I needed to hurt myself. I carried on hitting the corner of my diary against my head and thighs, hoping to quench that thirst I had for physical pain. Then I went into the bathroom, and tore off the plaster holding the tube into my nose. I wanted to rip out the tube but something stopped me. I don't know what it was. At the time I thought I was being weak, but I can see now that some part of me was being immensely strong. Some part of me was thinking, *"They'll only put it back in, and you promised not to put yourself through that again."*

Even more disappointed and angry, I went out to the desk and asked the male nurse to redo my nose plaster, saying it had got wet and come off. Once he had done it, I went back into my room, not knowing what to do. Lily was coming to visit me that afternoon, but not for an hour or so.

"I may as well try and burn off that orange," I thought. So I took a walk down the ward, going past rooms on one side and beds on the other. The ward was very long. There

was a big main desk in the middle of it where lots of different people were working and chatting. I didn't really give them a second thought as I skulked past them. I got to the end of the ward and stood at the door. Outside there was a large open landing with stairs leading up from the car park and a couple of vending machines. *"So that's where Dad goes to get his 7Up,"* I thought. There was an intercom-style button to let people in and out. My next thought was, *"I could get out. I could just go,"*

"And then what?" came a voice in my head. *"You can barely walk. You're here to get better, so why run away? Stop trying to run away, what are you so afraid of?"* I hadn't heard such a sensible voice for a very long time – not one of mine, anyway. At that moment though, I couldn't appreciate it, and it just angered me. Surprise, surprise.

I turned back, and just paced up and down the ward a bit. I went past an old lady's room, and she had some Fortisips on her table, a vase of flowers and a packet of digestives. She looked scary, she was skeletal. Her face was sunken and her eyes looked really big, like they would fall out of her face at any minute. I wondered what was wrong with her, and if she thought anything about me.

As I walked back towards my room, Nina and the male nurse were sat behind the desk. Nina caught my eye and gestured.

"Come and sit with me."

I thought, I may as well, as I didn't exactly have anything else to do. I went to sit next to her and she pushed a jewellery magazine in front of me.

"Which ones do you like?" she asked.

I really wasn't interested at all. This is not what I'm like normally, but anorexia seems to throw a veil over everything – that special brightness and curiosity of life just isn't there any more. And if it was, I wasn't allowed to enjoy it. But I flicked through the magazine and pointed vaguely at bits and pieces. Somehow, she got me chatting again and told me what she was doing over the school holiday with her sons (she had two). She was going to take them to the playground.

While we were talking, Lily arrived! I was so happy to see her. I walked towards her and hugged her, and then we went into my room. She'd brought me some oranges and an Arroword book, and another magazine – I think it was Look or something like that. She asked me how I was. *"Where do I start?"* I thought.

"I'm OK," I said. I didn't really know what I should say, whether to be honest and risk scaring her? Or just leave it there.

"It's hard – but I'm OK." I was sitting up in bed and she was in the big chair. She sent me love from some other friends and said they'd like to visit me, if that was all right with me. My instinctive thought was just *"Why? Why would they want to visit me?"*

We ended up doing an Arroword for a bit. Then it all just got too much for me. I started thinking about my friends, and how far away from them I was. I was jealous that they were out living their lives and I was trapped. Trapped by my own feelings, my own actions. Lily could see I was upset.

"Hey, why don't you get into bed? You look tired."

"Yeah, yeah, I am sorry..."

She helped me into bed and pulled the blanket over me. I started to cry and she held my hand in both of hers, and said gently,

"It's OK." She looked worried, but so understanding. Steady and brave. I felt awful, like I'd let her down.

"I'm sorry."

"You don't need to be sorry."

"It's just ... I'm really lonely. I'm just so far away from every-one. I wish I could be with my family."

"I know, it must be really hard. You're being so brave. We're all so proud of you."

"What is there to be proud of?" I thought. *"I'm weak, and the reason I'm here is because I failed."* I don't even remember what I was trying to do, but I definitely failed.

"Thank you so much." I just lay there and cried. I was really tired, so I closed my eyes. I felt so bad for letting Lily down. I wanted so much to show her I was OK and really trying – but I just couldn't. I wanted to be fun and entertaining for her, I didn't want to bring her down or make her sad. I wanted to be there for her and be a good friend. But I couldn't.

As I lay there with my eyes closed, I heard Lily start to cry. This broke my heart.

"You've made your friend cry now. She's there for you and all you can do is make her cry," said the voice in my head. Now I couldn't bear to open my eyes. We sat there until a nurse came in and said it was the end of visiting time. I was relieved for Lily so that she could get away.

"*I've got to go, Grace,*" she said.

"*Oh, OK,*" I said, opening my eyes. "*Thank you so much for coming.*"

"*I'll text you in the week to see when I can come next, and maybe bring Ailish?*"

"*She wants to come back??*" Said my head.

"*Yeah, that would be lovely,*" I said out loud. She said goodbye and left I was too sad to even be angry. I slept for a while after that; I was very tired.

When I woke up, I felt slightly happier. I got up and opened my curtains. I remember it being a very bright afternoon. I texted my mum asking if she could come alone when she came to visit in the evening. She was meant to be coming with Emily, but I felt like talking to Mum alone, properly.

Nina came in a couple of times. She offered me some tea, which I said no to, politely and apologetically.

"*Are you sure? Try some soup,*" she said – but it was no use.

"*I'm going to have a cup of coffee when the tea lady comes round,*" I said. This didn't really please her, and she persisted, but had no joy. She asked me what I was doing and I think I was watching a DVD. Then she asked me about my hobbies and what I liked to do at home. I couldn't really answer her. All that "home" was for me was a place to hide. "Home" was my room. I was too scared to be anywhere else in case there was food around, or people I didn't know, who might judge me; or mum and dad trying to get me to eat. I had spare time, but I couldn't for the life of me tell Nina what I did with it.

"I like crosswords."

Nina made a face. *"Do you like knitting?"* she asked.

This reminded me of a holiday I went on a couple of years before with my oldest friend, Katie. She came with my family to stay for a few days with my grandparents in Wales, for my birthday. And over the few days we were there, Katie and I learnt to knit. We did it avidly – on the beach, in bed, in the garden, sitting on the bench over-looking the bay. It brought back really great memories, reminding me of times when things seemed so much simpler, so much more innocent.

"Actually," I told Nina, *"I do know how to knit. But I haven't done it for years."*

"Right. I will bring you a book I have; it's all about sewing, knitting and stitching."

This made me smile, and feel really special and considered.

"Oh. Thank you."

Then I texted my mum, asking her to bring some knitting things. I thought I could at least make something as I had a lot of time on my hands. I was feeling a lot calmer now, more clear-headed and relaxed than I had been for a while.

When mum came, we sat in my room, knitting, and I introduced her to Nina. Then Nina asked if I wanted some ice cream, and I said, *"No, thank you."* She rolled her eyes and came closer to my bed, putting her hand on my shoulder gently. I hugged her round her waist and she said,

"Why not? Just have a little bit of ice cream for me?"

I smiled. *"I'm not ready. I am trying, but I'm not ready."*

"Fine, fine. But by the time I next see you, I hope you'll have something."

"When are you next here?" I asked bravely.

"Um, Friday."

"Right."

"Will you have some ice cream on Friday?"

"Yes, I'll try."

Now this was bizarre. I had just welcomed the idea of food, this idea of willingly eating food. And not some kind of low-fat crackerbread – ice cream! OK, so it wasn't like accepting it then and there, but even agreeing to at some point in the near future, was such a huge step. And it felt great!

I didn't want to make a big deal of it, just in case. So I quietly had a cheeky high-five with myself in my head, and Nina left me to be with Mum. After we had been sitting for a while, knitting, I said to Mum,

"I think I grew up too quickly."

"What makes you say that?" She sounded a little surprised.

"Well, I'm only sixteen, and look at me. I've been in a serious relationship with someone two years older than me for over 18 months. Maybe I wasn't ready for that. I'm too young for that, surely."

Thinking about that holiday with Katie, it had got me thinking about my relationship with Dan, and that summer before I started going out with him. I spent loads of time with my friends from primary school, and I remember just being so happy, and worrying about so little, and I missed it. I felt like I'd lost that part of myself. Things had got so complicated and tangled up in knots – the real me was in there somewhere, and I was on my way to release her – sword in hand.

"That's interesting," said my mum. *"What's made you think about that?"*

"Knitting." I smiled. *"I've just been thinking about that summer and how happy I was. I miss it."* Then I told her *"I've had a couple of cups of Nescafe today, and that reminded me of grandma's house."*

Mum smiled. *"That's great."*

I hadn't let myself have tea or coffee for a long time, so this was a really big step for me. But I know mum and I didn't want to make a big deal of it, just in case. I remember being very relaxed that evening – a world away from the place I'd been hours before.

Hadfield 1 *Liz*

27/3/08 10:03 to Seth:
I talked to her this morning and she almost sounded like herself. She saw a doctor and dietician this morning and so things are moving. I'm going up with Em tonight and dad's going up tomorrow if you want to join him x thanks for going, I'll pay you for the hottie! X

27/3/08 16:01 from Seth:
I've just left now actually, she's much more herself today which was so lovely to see. She asked me to warn you that she'll be just starting her first tube feeding session as you arrive tonight so be prepared x x x

16:28 to Grace:
Hey love are you OK with em coming tonight or would you rather just me? S told me abt the tube feeding x love you loads x x

16:57 from Grace:
would love for emily to come ☺ I miss her loads x x

Once Grace was in Hadfield 1, I felt that she would be looked after. The atmosphere was very calm and cheerful. She had her own room but people popped in and out. There were named nurses allocated to her. I still thought about her constantly, worried about what would happen next, whether they would transfer her to Leeds, but at least something was being done to stop the terrible frightening decline of her body.

The doctors and nurses would not tell me anything about Grace's treatment, which I found very frustrating. I appreciated that she was over 16, and was being treated like an adult – but she was so fragile, and she would be the first to agree she was not really herself. As her family, all we knew about what the medical team planned for her, was what we heard from Grace, or Anorexic-Grace.

Martha was fantastic. She talked to me and let me know a little of how Grace was and what treatment was being planned. She was always calm and restrained.

I was terrified of the prospect of tube feeding. The last memory I have of my mother is of her lying in a hospital bed with a tube in her nose and horrible beigey-pink gloop being pumped into her.

I was ten. I didn't know if the stuff was going in or out. It was horrible. Over thirty years later, I knew that it was not logical, just an emotional reaction, but I knew that seeing Grace with a tube in her nose might be too hard to bear. It would look, to me, as though she was edging closer, unstoppably, to death, even though the opposite was true. I was so glad when I went in and saw her. She was sitting up in bed. The tube was quite narrow and unobtrusive compared to my mother's. The fluid was whitish, a much less repulsive colour. She looked ill. She looked scarily thin. But she did not look like my mother losing her fight against cancer.

The things I've quoted and described here are just part of our lives at this time. Ed and I were both working full time, and so was Seth. Looking back, I question my determination to go to work every day but the culture of our organisation was very anti-absence and it was part of my job to enforce that. I worried about the financial consequences of taking time off, especially when I thought there would come a time when I was commuting to Leeds to visit Grace. Tilly was at primary school and Emily at secondary. I tried, not always successfully, to spend time with both of them talking about and doing things that did not revolve around Grace and her illness. I wanted them to know that my connection with them was not threatened by Grace needing so much of my time and attention.

The pain of Grace being so ill was a constant presence, companion to a continuing "normal" life. Our schedule now had to include travel and hospital visits and making sure there was change for the hospital parking meters as well as making sure that we didn't run out of food and clean clothes and the dog got walked. Other interests fell by the wayside. Many of the texts I've not included were me sending my apologies, yet again, for choir or yoga – two things I love and help me to cope.

Turning the Corner *Grace*

Monday 31st March

That morning I was woken by nurses Hazel and Sarah, which meant I had slept a little that night. They wanted to weigh me. I was very willing to be weighed as well. But as they helped me out of bed, my body ached. My skin felt thin and every touch was a hammer through my body.

They helped me into the weighing scales, which looked like a wheelchair with no wheels. As I sat down, I felt the bones which were meant to be cushioned by my bum, digging into the chair's seat, and I started to cry.

"I'm sorry darling, we've got to do this," said Hazel firmly.

"No, it's not that. It really hurts," I cried.

"Well, you can get up now."

They helped me back into bed, and filled in the file.

"Have I lost any more weight?" I asked. For the first time in longer than I can remember, I wanted the answer to be *"No".* If I had lost more weight, what would the past week of hell have been for? Anorexia was not going to win.

"No, you haven't, Grace," Hazel didn't smile as she said this. She looked concerned and very busy. *"You haven't gained any either, but that's not surprising."*

I was proud. I was too scared to show it, but I felt good that I had maintained my weight, miniscule as it was. I'd maintained it for a week. My aim in life since September had been to lose weight, and it was very strange to let that change, to let myself change inside and out.

"OK, well, Dr Harrington's back today, so he'll be coming to see you at about 10.30," Hazel said as she sorted out my medicines and my tube. She was less stressed now.

"These really are rank," I smiled, as I popped the various pills into my mouth, and then the tiny plastic syringe of Prozac.

"I know love, but you need them."

"Yeah, I know. It's all helping me get better." I smiled at her.

When Dr Harrington came to my room, he was followed by four young, very smart-looking doctors, and Hazel, who stood at the foot of my bed with her hands folded together like you have to stand for school photos.

Dr Harrington was very intimidating. He was a bit shab-by-looking, very tall and thin, with a tired face and dark hair. His eyes were a grey shade of blue, I think – he looked a bit like The Demon Headmaster – very serious. He introduced himself and explained why he'd been away and so on. Then he began asking me questions: what I ate? Why? Would I eat any more? Why?

I don't think he made eye contact once while he spoke to me. There was no interest in his expression or tone of voice. His attitude was purely business.

"And you're..." flipping through my file, *"16?"*

"Yes."

"Very young. And you're what, at school? College?"

"Well, um, I left school to come into here. To get better."

"Right. Yes, And how long do you plan to be here?"

This threw me. I hadn't even considered leaving hospital. I mean, I'd spent the past week longing to see my family but I hadn't considered the idea of being well enough to go home. The fact I was there, in a hospital bed, was the only thing that helped me recognise that I was ill. So that when anorexia told me I wasn't good enough, or that I should try harder, I could say, *"Look I'm in hospital. I'm dangerously thin and I'm unwell. This is your fault, not mine. Fuck off!"* I didn't know how to answer the question.

"*Um, I don't know.*" I felt angry with him. "*I hadn't really thought about it.*"

"*Well, haven't you got exams to be preparing for?*"

I'd had enough of that. I didn't want to hear about exams or revision, couldn't he see there were more important things to worry about? I felt like crying.

"*I don't know if I'm going back to school. I really just want to concentrate on getting better right now,*" I fought back. I wasn't shouting, but I felt very defensive.

"*Of course, I'm just trying to get a time span here. Our aim here is to get you to a healthy enough weight for you to go home as quickly as possible.*" He spoke in a deep, matter-of-fact way.

"*Right. I'm really trying. I really am.*" I almost pleaded with him. I looked at Hazel for some kind of backup but she just looked at the floor. He then asked me something about ice-skating, which I found very odd. I used to ice-skate until about the end of Year 10. I loved it and I was quite good at it. It became really hard to keep going because I lived quite far from the rink, and my coach moved away so I failed one of my exams. I lost quite a lot of confidence after that.

I don't know if Dr Harrington had been told by Hazel or my mum or someone that I used to skate, and I can't really remember what he even said, just that it was about skating and I found it very strange for him to mention it.

"OK," he went on, *"so we'll carry on with the tube feed, and slowly increase that as your body gets used to it. And you'll be seeing the dietician this afternoon, all being well. I think we're looking at around the end of April for you to be ready for home."* He was very matter-of-fact. He gestured to the following doctors for them to leave, and nodded at me as he followed them out.

"Ok, thank you," I said, softly.

After that, the usual morning things went on, lots of cleaning. Some nurses came in to change my bed and I talked to them as they did. We looked at my pictures and they wouldn't believe me when I told them it was me.

"You look very beautiful there."

"I was. And now look at me..."

"Hey, you are beautiful, there's no reason you can't look like that again though." And she had a point – it made me think. What was stopping me from being beautiful again?

I really liked that nurse – I think her name was Jenny. She was from the Philippines. She helped me back into bed after making my bed, because my body was feeling so drained and raw. I felt everything so severely through my thin skin. Debbie the tea lady came round a couple of times and we chatted. I had a cup of coffee and felt fine about it. I remember just feeling very relaxed, and welcoming people in to talk – everyone: cleaners, nurses, and nobody ignored me; nobody said they had to rush off – it was so lovely.

The dietician lady came in to talk to me after lunch, while everyone was resting; so all the curtains were drawn. She came and sat by my bed and asked how I was. I told her I was feeling a lot happier and was drinking tea and coffee – and she was really pleased. She was just genuinely enthusiastic about me feeling better. It was so encouraging, and just made me feel ten times better.

"So, as you're drinking more of a variety now – how would you feel about something like milk as an aim?"

I thought about it.

"Yeah, ... yeah, I could do that..." I smiled.

"Brilliant. Well, I'm up here again on Friday, so shall we say we'll increase the night time feed and in the mean time you can work towards maybe having a glass of milk?"

"Yes. Definitely."

"Fantastic."

It was visiting time, and people started walking about, then my friend Katie and her mum appeared at my door – Katie was holding a huge bunch of flowers.

"Ooh, looks like you've got some visitors" the dietician said as she picked up her bag to go. *"I'm really glad to see how well you're doing, Grace. Keep it up!"* She smiled very happily, and left to go and talk to Hazel outside my room.

I beckoned Katie and her mum to come in. She looked a bit nervous, understandably, but was smiling. I thanked her for the flowers and then she told me all about her French exchange she'd just got back from – she'd been working in a florist's. They were really beautiful flowers and it was nice to see something so bright and natural in that sterile environment. After we'd spoken for a bit, her mum went and sat in the TV room while me and Katie talked some more. We spoke about that holiday in Wales, knitting, and she'd brought me some Lady Grey teabags (my favourite) with a ribbon round them.

"Your mum said you were enjoying tea and coffee again," she said, *"so I thought you might like a bit of variety."*

When it was getting on for time for them to leave, Katie's mum came back in and sat down next to her.

"How are you, Grace?"

I smiled. It was my instinct to smile, and I did.

"I'm feeling positive. I really feel like I'm going somewhere, and that I am going to get better."

"That's really great," She smiled back. There was a bit of a pause, and I just looked at Katie, and thought about where I was and what I'd done to myself – and suddenly felt scared. Like this wonderful peace I had might be taken away by the terrifying thing that had taken over me for the last few months. I started to cry.

"I don't want to die. I really don't want to die."

"Grace, you're not going to die! Look how well you're doing!" Katie said. I could see she was upset but was being the brave person I needed her to be. *"You clearly want to get better, and you will."*

This helped my fear subside and I agreed with her. There was no point in dwelling on why and whose fault it was, because it would have only fed every anxiety in the horrible cycle.

"I will get better, when I do can we go to Wales again?" I said, wiping my tears away.

"Yeah." Katie smiled and held my hand. After they'd left I wrote in my diary, which I had tried a few times since being in hospital but I'd torn out the pages when I got angry.

I wrote about how I felt so proud of myself, and how I deserved some love, and how incredible the nurses in the hospital were. Also how proud Martha, Rachel and Rowena would be. I also wrote that I was *"Ready to change inside and out"*. That was such a huge step! It was so brave – to say that I had the self-belief and confidence to change my ways. The way I thought and acted, to make myself a better person. I also wrote, *"I'm not completely happy, I know there's things I have to sort out"*, which shows I did still have the perspective of not thinking everything was perfect and wonderful suddenly. But I was the happiest I'd been in longer than I could remember.

Later on I was talking to Hazel about drinking some more different things and I agreed to try out some different Fortisips. I felt very brave indeed – sipping up chocolate, raspberry and a fruit/syrup combo, which was not very enjoyable. But I drank them! And I didn't get thrown in to a fit of anger and depression after it. In fact, I think I did some knitting. Then my mum rang the ward to see how I was doing and Hazel let me talk to her. I remember saying, *"Mum, I've had an epiphany – I'm going to get better."*

"Really?" she said, half playfully/half worried.

"Yeah. I actually am! I can do it."

"That's brilliant, darling."

I smiled so much that day. In the evening, before my dad arrived to visit me, one of the cleaners who I'd kind of spoken to before came in.

"Hello, come in!" I smiled and welcomed him in. *"What's your name?"*

"I'm Mohammed. What's yours?"

"I'm Grace. It's nice to meet you. Thanks for cleaning my room." We chatted for a bit about why I was there and everything, and as he was finishing he asked me if I was going to eat soon, and I said very calmly with a smile on my face, *"No, I'm not ready."*

"What if I brought you the best pizza in the world?"

"Is it really the best?"

"You wouldn't be able to say no!"

"Well, if it's the best ..."

"If I bring you one now, would you eat it?" He grinned, and looked like he might actually go and retrieve one.

"I'm not hungry."

"You are hungry, you just don't know it." That made me think. I'd spent such a long time ignoring my own needs and feelings. I couldn't imagine the decadence of thinking *"I'm hungry"* and then actually eating something I felt like.

My dad arrived then and I introduced him to Mohammed. He sat down by my bed and told me how well I looked and seemed. Then out of his bag he got a bag of oranges – as per – and THEN... a bunch of grapes! And you know what? I didn't freak out! I was a bit shocked by his bravery and again, welcomed the idea of eating them.

We chatted for a bit and then I got really tired and closed my eyes. While I was resting, Seth came in and I woke up a bit to say hello. He said he could notice as soon as he came in

"Even when you had your eyes closed. You just look brighter," he smiled.

"I feel it. I just feel happy."

We all talked for a while, and while we did I got Dad to peel an orange for me – HUGE. I also ate a few grapes – only about three, but as I did, I was thinking *"How am I getting away with this? Why aren't I freaking out? Where is the horrible little bat animal telling me I'm awful? What's going on?"* But I didn't want to think about it too much. In case it caught me.

"When I get better, can we go for an Everest please?" I remember asking, getting excited. That's our favourite Indian restaurant. I saw Dad and Seth exchange a look of utter joy and amazement and shock, then quickly hide it and play it cool.

"Yes, of course."

Then we talked about the future; I told them I didn't want to carry on at sixth form, and Dad was so supportive.

"Fine. You always wanted to go to college anyway."

It felt so simple – doing what I wanted to do. Why wouldn't I? Why shouldn't I? Why had I been trying so hard to please everyone but myself?

"I've been thinking about all the things I could do when I get better, like getting a job! I could get a job in an actual shop like Topshop or Starbucks."

"Grace, you can do anything," they told me. And, I believed them. I honestly believed that life was so much bigger than the hideous stupid voice in my head telling me I wasn't good enough. There was a whole world out there full of beautiful, exciting experiences that I could, and would, be a part of.

Once they'd left and said their goodbyes, my night nurse came in. He was one I'd not met before. He asked if I wanted a bowl for my fruit - I hadn't hidden it away so it was still on the table. Then he came back with the bowl and arranged the fruit in it very nicely. Then he started sorting out my feed and I asked him what he was called, where he was from, what he liked doing, etc. He had such an interesting life! His name was Patch and he came from the Bahamas. I think he had something like 13 brothers and sisters who still all live there. He told me how he really liked being active. He had a fold-up bike he takes everywhere with him so he was very fit and didn't need a car. And he told me all about these adventure cruises he goes on, where they get up at 6 in the morning and go hiking, climbing, diving, biking and then party all night on the ship.

He had such an active life – and a great outlook on it. Just to grab it and go for it. I liked Patch a lot.

He said goodnight, but I wasn't feeling ready for sleep, so I watched a DVD and ate some more grapes as I did. But I couldn't concentrate on it properly. There were too many things going on in my head – it felt like there were cogs turning and things just falling into place. So much was going on in my head, yet I wasn't saying a word. It was a feeling I'd never experienced before – almost like I was in a trance. All the thoughts that had popped into my head over the past few days; all of the tiny yet huge realisations just all came flooding into my mind. And it just made sense. It's very hard to explain. I've spent so long trying to find a way of explaining what exactly happened that night. It was like a kind of presence or being patted me on the back and said, *"Hi, I'm here for you. You are a wonderful person. Go for it. Be wonderful."* Suddenly I had someone to say it all to.

"I'm sorry. I'm so sorry, I've been awful. I screwed up. But I made it – look, I'm here and you didn't let me and my family give up. I nearly did. I thought I had, but you didn't. And my family wouldn't let me, they're not going to lose me. I'm going to live. Thank you."

How could I have been so awful? I've been such a demon. All the people who love me …

Dan …

They didn't give up on me, and I won't, I am going to live.

And right then, all of those emotions just erupted inside of me – I had butterflies that would give anything to fly right out of my mouth.

I'll say now, that this may well have been a simple reaction to the Prozac and extra calories in my system, but it felt like more. It's very easy to say my starved system was processing new chemicals. I'm sure an element of it was that. But I know that something in the way I think and feel changed that night. I felt my heart get a little lighter.

I turned on my light and looked at my lovely full fruit bowl and ate. Not hastily. One grape at a time. It was almost too much for all the senses in my mouth. It was so alien – the texture and taste, the feel and smell of something that wasn't an orange – my mouth didn't know what to do!

As I was eating, I understood what Mo had said; I was hungry, I just didn't know it. Well, I knew it then, and I ate.

I couldn't believe what was happening, but at the same time I knew so strongly that I had changed. I felt so secure of myself and the love I had around me. It was a faith I didn't know I had, bigger than self-belief or good self esteem. It all felt bigger than me. I knew people wouldn't trust me – they had no reason to – but I have never been so sure of anything in my entire life. Another voice that popped into my head as I was getting to know my tongue again, said,

"What if I get fat?"

To this, I actually laughed out loud. And carried on eating. I looked at the picture I had by my bed of me and Emily and Tilly on holiday in Spain. And I could truly see how beautiful I was. I looked healthy and happy and I wanted to look like that again. Why couldn't I? There was nothing stopping me – I felt powerful.

Patch popped his head round my door to check I was all right and I told him I was fine, and could I have a drink of Ovaltine to help me sleep. When he came back I chatted to him a bit more and asked him if he believed in God.

"Not really. I think there's so much sadness in the world, how could he exist?" He said this quite matter-of-factly and I nodded.

"I understand". I did understand. I tried to work out what I'd found myself.

During the night, I ate the whole bunch of grapes and most of the two bags of oranges, and I didn't feel guilty – I felt proud! Completely, deeply proud. I stayed up for a long time: I couldn't sleep, knowing how wonderful the world was. I texted my auntie Gill; I remember asking her to call me as soon as she could in the morning because I wanted to talk to her. I wanted to tell her how amazing I felt and how I was going to get so much better and be beautiful again. I wanted everyone to know. I'd found something immensely special and precious, I couldn't contain it. All the happiness and joy was just building and building inside me and I didn't know what to do with it! Eventually Patch talked me into lying down and trying to get some sleep. I couldn't lie down flat because of the feed, but I did manage to get to sleep. Before I did, I lay with my eyes closed and prayed.

"Thank you."

Gill rang in the morning before breakfast had started on the ward. I told her everything that had happened in the past few days, trying to stay calm as I did, but I couldn't. Before I knew it, I was crying down the phone to her, happily of course but quite hysterical. I remember her sounding worried. I didn't want people to worry any more. I felt safe and really happy and I just wanted people to be happy for me. It's completely understandable that she was worried though, and all that I could do was try to reassure her. I had to go, because breakfast was coming round and I wasn't going to miss that!

The trolley arrived at my door and the ladies had realised something was going on. They were smiling as they asked if I wanted any breakfast.

"Yes! Yes! I do!" I shrieked. I had cornflakes with sugar. It didn't taste great, to be honest, well, it was only corn-flakes, after all. There was still something very comforting about the familiarity of the taste, texture, everything. Then I had some cooked breakfast – sausage, toast and tinned tomatoes, which was also a bit ropey, but I wasn't complaining. What did I have to complain about?! Nothing. I felt on top of the world and everyone on the ward seemed to be so happy for me. Instead of glancing worriedly into my room, nurses were smiling and chatting to me. Suddenly I wasn't in this bubble any more, I'd broken through the unbreakable glass and set myself free. I didn't consider questioning it, because I felt so sure of my new point of view and perspective.

I remember talking that day. As well as eating! I kept my door open as much as I could, and texted Rowena and Lily saying I'd like to see them and that I was feeling a lot better. Mum was coming to visit in the afternoon and I texted her asking her to bring edible treats. I can't explain how excited I was to see my family. And hug them, and thank them. Just to share space and time with them again was all I could wish for. I had a shower as the ward was being cleaned, and really enjoyed it. Afterwards I got dressed in some jogging bottoms and a vest top – but I didn't like how I could see every bone I had in my chest, so I put a tee-shirt over it. I saw the good-looking cleaner, Eddie, and went to speak to him, and I remember I felt really tall. I was standing my full height, with my head up, and I wasn't ashamed. I'd forgotten that I was tall – that sounds silly, but I had. I'd ignored everything about myself except the things I hated for so long. It was like meeting up with an old friend and wondering why you'd lost touch, because the real me was actually a funny, friendly, pretty person, who didn't deserve all the mean things I used to say to myself. I was finding myself again, the girl who was in the pictures by my bed was still there, she just got lost.

When the news trolley made its way down the ward, I spent all the money I had on chocolate and biscuits – it was so exciting. I couldn't believe that I was allowed to eat anything I wanted, so I went for a little walk to find a doctor just to check. I found one of the pretty young doctors from Dr Harrington's team, and asked her.

"Yep. Anything you feel like! If you're happy to eat, go for it!" She smiled, as though it was plain and clear – which it was!

I couldn't believe my luck. Anything I wanted – amazing!

At lunch I had a full dinner, and cake for pudding – which made me realise eating with a tube down my throat was a little bit uncomfortable – but that wasn't going to stop me.

I got so excited waiting for my mum to arrive. I walked down to the main doors and back again quite a few times. Then when I was stood outside my room talking to some nurses, I saw her coming down the ward. My heart nearly jumped out of my mouth and as soon as I glimpsed her I tried to run up to her. This wasn't a very good idea, as I'd momentarily forgotten my malnourished body wasn't capable of doing something like that. So I ended up crashing to the floor, which was very painful because of my skeletal figure. I felt everything. But I didn't care, I had my mum.

Everyone crowded round and helped me up and I put my arm around mum and we went into my room. She'd brought me some real treats from Waitrose – cookies, strawberries and little brioches. I started explaining to her as best I could how great I was feeling, as I ate. She just looked terrified.

"Mum, why can't you be happy for me? This is great!" I was annoyed that she couldn't trust me, but of course she couldn't. She had spent six months trying to get me to cheer up and eat. And there I was – cheery and eating!

"I'm just worried, darling. If you are getting better that's fantastic – but what if you come down from this high? How hard are you going to fall? It's just hard to believe, that's all."

I did understand, but I was better! I just wanted to see her happy. I tried to reassure her.

"I understand completely, I wouldn't believe it. But I do. I feel like something's changed inside me". I said this in a purposefully calmer tone, gesturing to my heart. *"I trust this. It's real, I promise. And I'm just going to prove to you that it is, so you have nothing to worry about."*

"OK." She still looked terrified.

I can't really remember what else we talked about, but I do remember hugging her, and just feeling so com-fortable and safe. I hadn't hugged my mum properly in so long. I hated being touched before, it made my skin crawl. But now I craved it, feeling someone else's skin touch mine, and now I'd started to warm up as well it was even nicer. My hands were still chilly but the rest of me felt comfortably warm. That alone made me feel really relaxed and less tense. I rang dad off Mum's phone and played a trick on him, pretending to be Mum saying I'd gone off the wall – not very tasteful I know but I just wanted to have a laugh. Then I asked him seriously to bring a pizza tonight so we could share it for tea.

"Will you actually eat it?" I could imagine his face frowning with doubt.

"Yes, I promise! Of course I will!" I knew he wouldn't believe it until he saw me, but he agreed in the end. I told him how great I was feeling and how excited I was about seeing him later on, then mum spoke to him. She was still looking really uneasy and worried, which hurt – because now I was worried I'd not proved to her that I was feeling like Grace again.

"I'll just stick to it, carry on getting better and then I can give her the happiness she deserves," I thought to myself.

That afternoon I think was when Megan and Lily rang me. They were together at Megan's house and I remember crying to them, thanking them and apologising and say-ing how I couldn't wait to see them. We agreed they'd come the next day at 2 and bring me some goodies. I loved the idea of my friends being excited to see me, and instead of me thinking I was too boring for them or that I'd just bring them down, I was excited too! Everything felt simple, I wasn't worrying about "what ifs" and "when", it was here and now, and I was going to make the most of it.

When Dad came that evening, he brought a Meat Feast, which we shared. I told him all about what I'd been feeling, how I wanted to carry on, and he asked me what I was going to do about Dan.

"I don't want to be with him any more." I said it very calmly because I knew it was right. I'd wanted it for a while but just not felt able to finish it. *"I need to be on my own, to find the girl I am."*

Dad nodded, he understood. Then he asked me about school and exams, what I wanted to do about them and I said I didn't want to go back. And, surprisingly, he agreed with me.

I was feeling a lot calmer than when mum had been in earlier – just as happy, only calmer. We talked about the summer, and what we could do. I could get a job, apply for college, celebrate my birthday in Wales again, and burn my dressing gown! I'd lived in it practically since Christmas, because I'd been so cold all the time. I suddenly had a pang of guilt thinking about how much I must have cost them on the heating bill.

"So what are you aiming for, weight-wise?" Dad asked me.

"I want to just be how I was before. I was beautiful and healthy and that's all I want."

"You really were beautiful. And you had a gorgeous figure, you don't want to be all straight and narrow like Ikea Knightley."

This made me laugh – it was so nice to laugh with Dad again. We talked over some of the things I'd worried about before that made me feel sad – things with the family, Deirdre, school. And once I actually said them out loud, they really did sound silly. He put me at ease about them very easily, and I was so willing to accept the nice truths about myself; this was rare – and it felt great! Things just felt simpler now. I was important to myself and I wasn't ashamed to indulge in that. When it was time for Dad to go, I gave him a big hug goodbye, which was lovely.

I was just getting ready for bed after he'd gone and my chest started feeling fluttery. My hands were tingling and I felt really shaky; I didn't understand what was going on at all because in my head I felt fine. My body was panicking yet my mind was calm. I thought maybe I needed some sugar so drank some lucozade, but it didn't help. I went to go and find Patch to see if he knew what I should do. I started to walk down the award but then my legs stopped working – they literally just froze and I stood there like I was stuck in the mud! Luckily Patch came down and I explained what was going on, and he didn't know what the problem could be but he still put me at ease. We managed to escort my failing feet back to my bed and we started up the feed. Eventually I got back to normal by lying very still, just breathing. It was a big shock, that turn, but it brought me down to earth a bit I think. It helped me realise that although I felt invincible, I really wasn't and I was still mentally and physically very vulnerable. I knew I was safe; I just needed to give myself time.

The next morning I wrote in my diary how proud of myself I was, and how strong I felt. It was like I was meeting myself again, and all the things I once had the confidence to feel and say and be were coming back to me. I was growing into a mixture of my own true self, who I knew before but with a new outlook and perspective.

Martha came in the morning and I told her everything. I told her how great I felt and showed her my diary from the past few days. She was so happy for me: Martha had never been anything but supportive and understanding and nothing had changed. We talked for ages and I really enjoyed just being myself finally. It was a little like meeting her for the first time.

Ro and Lily visited me that afternoon – they brought me loads of goodies! Two big collages for my wall, a beautiful homemade card that said, *"We all (heart) Grace"* on the front, with glitter and everything. They also brought me the single best bacon sandwich I've ever had.

I think Dr Reed, the psychiatrist, came in that day as well. Naturally she thought my "good mood" was down to the Prozac. It upset me that she thought I wasn't genuine, but I understood her reaction.

That night, Mum and Emily brought me one of my old favourite dinners – couscous with veg and chicken, and Ben & Jerry's Phish Food ice cream. They also brought loads of nice nuts, fruits and things for breakfast. I was so excited to be able to enjoy food again – and eat really well. I wanted to be really good to my body – we definitely had some bridge-building to do.

I got mum to take pictures of me. I wanted to help people who were also affected by anorexia, I wanted to share my journey and experience with as many people as I could.

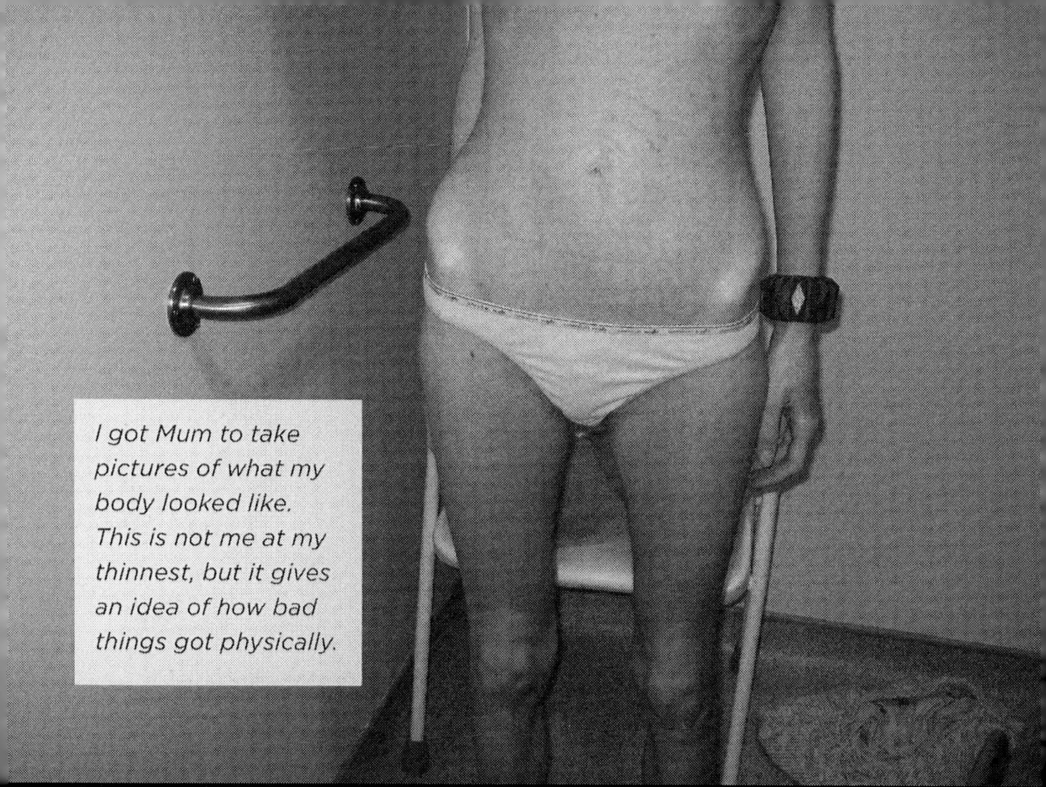

I got Mum to take pictures of what my body looked like. This is not me at my thinnest, but it gives an idea of how bad things got physically.

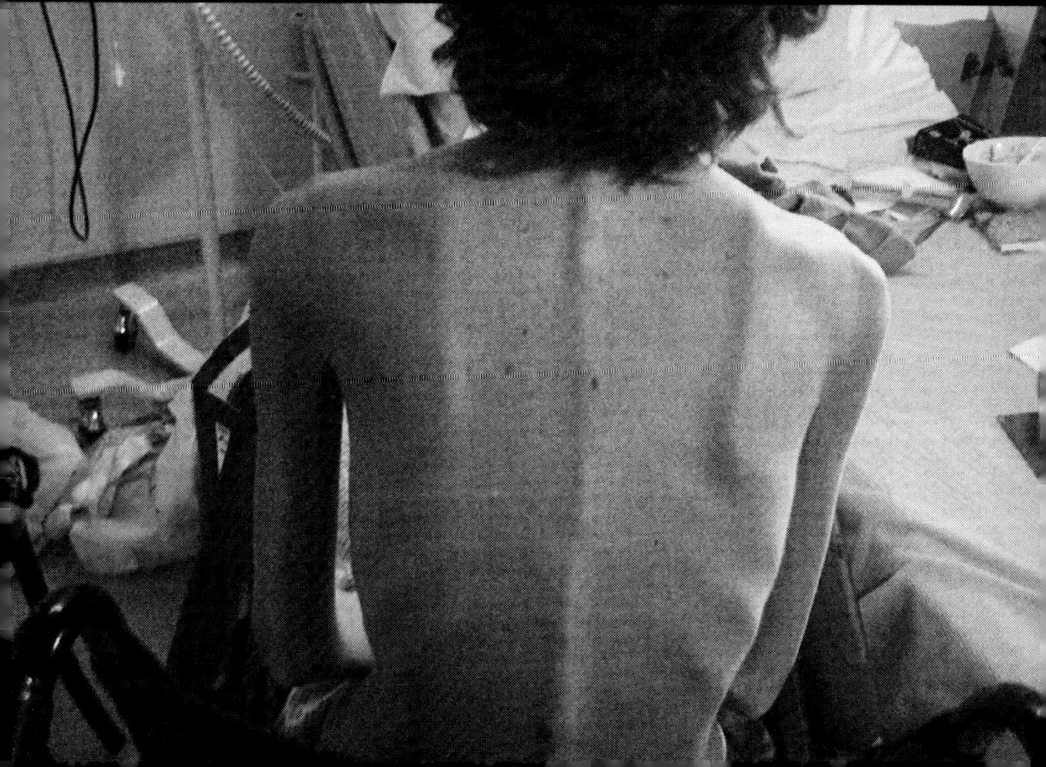

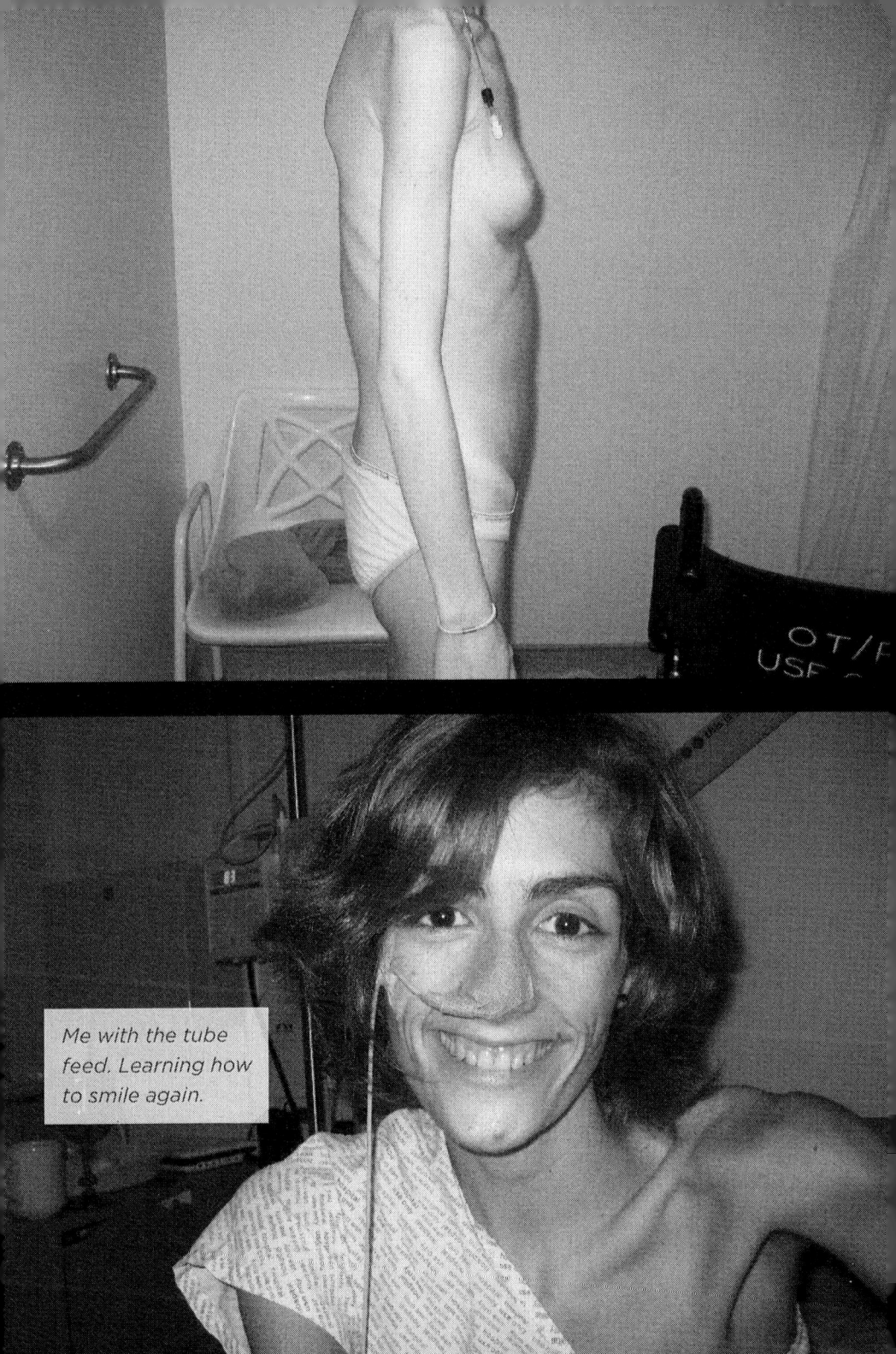

Me with the tube feed. Learning how to smile again.

It was so great seeing Emily again, laughing with her, catching up on her life, talking about friends and clothes and shoes – just being friends again.

After they left, I met a new night nurse called Veronica and we talked about each other's families, just got to know each other a bit. Then I went to the TV room to watch "House" with some of the older people off the ward. There was Norma, who was 66 – in fact it was her 66th birthday. She used to be a dinner lady. Then there was Tom, who was about 80 I think. He wasn't as lively as the others and didn't say much. Finally there was Vincent – he preferred being called Vinnie or Vin though. He was very funny and friendly; I think he had a soft spot for Norma. We talked all the way through "House" and all had hot chocolate and biscuits. I found out that Vin only lives round the corner from me – I never went round though. I can't remember what number it was. I was writing in my diary loads at this time, writing about all my new friends and everything I was feeling. I was just getting so much joy out of life and the mundane little tasks and exchanges with lovely people. I felt so confident, being nice to people was easy and simple there, and I felt like my positivity was actually helping people around me.

The next day I got weighed again. I was hoping I had gained weight. How quickly that became a believable thought in my mind is astonishing. In fact I would have been chuffed to have simply maintained what my weight was before – just to have some physical evidence of my determination and mental strength. On Monday 31st March – 41.3 kg. Thursday 3rd April – 45.6 kg!

The feeling I got when I saw that was a happiness that I couldn't explain. I was utterly overwhelmed by such a huge sense of pride. In the space of a week I'd gone from believing I was the most worthless, detestable being on Earth to actually feeling proud of myself. Proud of who I was, of everything I had achieved and what I was yet to achieve. And I wasn't scared any more! I knew so strongly that I was going to be OK. I felt a thousand feet tall, and nothing could change that.

I texted everyone in my phone book I was so happy. I got replies from people I really didn't expect, and they were all just genuine, honest expressions of support and happiness. I was still shocked that people actually cared. I thought I'd cut myself off so much that they wouldn't want anything to do with me. The doctors said that if I carried on progressing like that, I'd be able to go home by the end of the month! That motivated me a lot, the thought of being able to be with my family again.

Before my friends came in the afternoon, Dr O'Neill came in to meet me. She was the consultant psychiatrist who worked with SEDS. She had been away the whole time I'd been seeing Martha, so it was the first time I'd met her. She was very serious – not in a mean way, but she didn't smile once as I told her about the last few days. I explained how Nina helped me, and how I was changing and getting better as calmly as I could. But her point of view was totally clinical and she basically thought I'd gone even further off my rocker than I had been before. She said it was because of the Prozac that I was feeling so high, and warned me that I would want to do crazy wild things. She advised me to hide away my credit cards, not to eat excessively or at night, and... not to have sex! It really pissed me off how she reacted. She'd never met me before, though, and from the outside, that's how she was trained to react. I'd been touched by nothing short of a miracle, and miracles don't happen every day. I just had to justify myself by behaving as "sanely" as I possibly could. It was just so frustrating how cynical her attitude to me was. It really hurt to have someone tell me what I was feeling – something so powerful and beautiful – was wrong. I wrote some really mean things about her in my diary and it made me feel better, anyway!

Sceing Rachel, Ro, Megan and Joe that afternoon was brilliant. Rachel had brought me loads of presents from New York and we all ate chicken and chips together. They even brought in a blender so that I could make smoothies with all my tasty fruit. It was such a novelty just hanging out with my friends. Being able to hug them and just be – it was really comforting.

After they left, I just rested in my bed, watching a DVD. I don't think it was a particularly sad one, but something in it made me cry. And once I started I didn't stop. I literally didn't stop for at least an hour. I realised it was the first time I'd cried since all this brilliance had happened, and I really needed it. Just to release of all the emotion that was running through me.

Then I started thinking about Mum and Dad... what I'd put them through ... how scared they must have been. I felt deeply sad then. I knew that the way I'd behaved over the past six months wasn't entirely my fault, but part of me couldn't help but think *"What if...? What if I'd not joined the gym? What if I'd finished things with Dan earlier? What if I'd not talked to Rowena that night? What if I'd just let someone in?"* All of these things might or might not have changed how bad the situation got, and even now I still go over them in my mind. But it's pointless. And when I think about it properly, I genuinely wouldn't change a thing. Because the happiness, clarity and faith I have now is something so dear and invaluable, I treasure my perspective and my life because I know how special it is. I've learnt so much, and I'd hate to risk losing the outlook I have now.

I asked Dan to come in the next day, and speaking to him wasn't easy. I am so grateful to him for his unconditional love and support, and I won't write the details of what happened because it's between us. It was something that had to be done, and it's just a shame it was in such a bizarre setting. I feel awful that we didn't share my imme- diate recovery, purely because he'd been fighting for it so desperately. But it was time for it to be my journey.

I spent the next few days being quite boring really; I watched TV, ate lots of lovely food, saw my friends and family. I spent loads of time in the shower, moisturising and painting my nails and just enjoying my body. I had a new-found respect for it and loved taking care of it finally.

The first day that Tim was my nurse again, I was so happy to see him! I couldn't wait to show him how much better I was than when he'd last seen me. I really liked having him around on the ward, it was like having a friend there. And even when he was rushed off his feet he made sure I was OK. It meant a lot to me and I will never stop appre- ciating how lovely he was to me. He told me he'd ask if it would be OK to take the feed out, because I was back on real-people food I didn't need the tube any more.

The next day he took it out – it was really painful, and quite a sickly sensation – but it was 100% worth it. The sensation of being able to feel food go down my throat without the tube tugging and scratching – it was heaven.

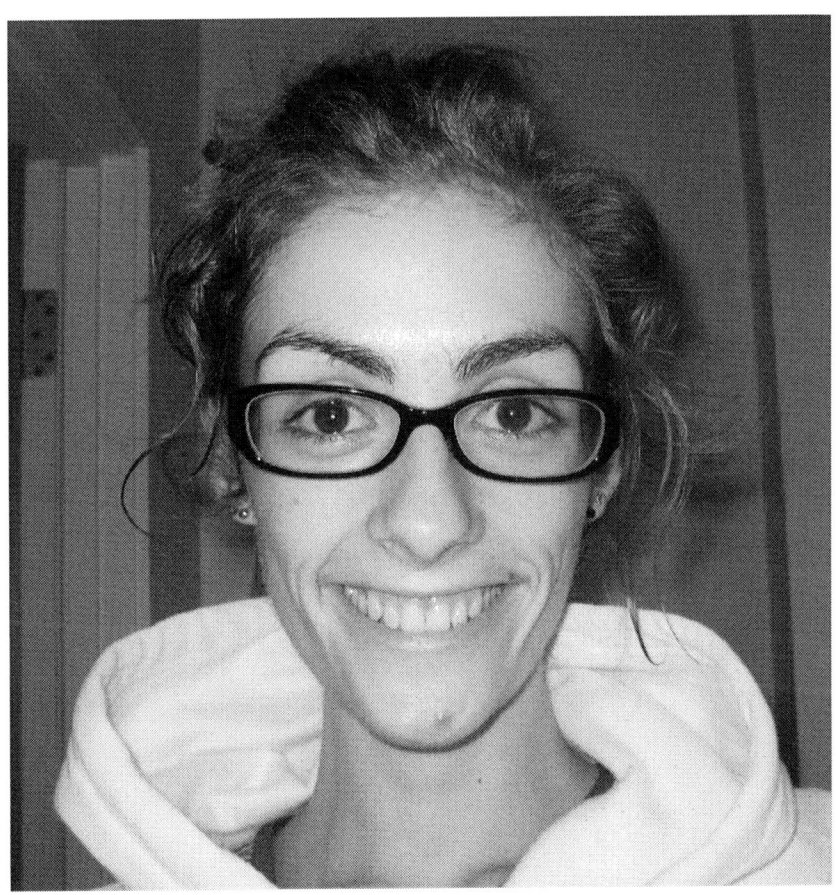

On Monday 7th April, I did the normal stuff – wrote to my grandparents, had breakfast and a shower. Then I saw the doctors on their rounds, and they said I might be able to home! That day! I remember saying,

"Yes, get me out of this bed! Let someone in who really needs it!" I was so excited – to be at home was all I wanted. I missed my family more than anything and the thought of being able to be around them again made me feel whole.

The doctors just needed to discuss everything with Martha and Dr O'Neill; this didn't make me feel very optimistic, as I knew Dr O still thought I was bipolar. I also knew Martha trusted me though, and whatever she decided would be best for me.

After I'd seen both of them, we all decided that I would go home the next day and Mum would stay at home with me for the next week. Because I had been very seriously ill, I still needed looking after. Lots of plans were also being made to ensure I would still get the care I needed, mentally. I 'd still visit Martha, a dietician, and another specialist to find out if my behaviour was related to some kind of bipolar syndrome. It felt really nice to know that I wasn't on my own. Having Martha, Dr O and my family all wanting this to be the beginning of a strong, safe recovery made me feel stronger and braver. I still knew what had happened was real and I was so determined to get my life back – that was my armour.

Tim kept an eye on me that day, and he was really busy, but still made the effort to come and chat. And he was really pushing for me to be able to go home as soon as possible, which I appreciated so much. I made him a card and used my new gold pen to decorate it. On the front it said *"I (heart) Tim"*. I think he was a bit embarrassed when I gave it to him – he blushed quite a lot!

My last night in hospital was actually really nice. And I was glad I got to have that time to prepare myself for going home, instead of just rushing off like I was escaping from jail. Because as much as my little room was lonely and detached from the real world – it was my place. I'd put all of my pictures up on my wall opposite my bed (which is apparently illegal!) and it looked amazing. Everyone who went past said how lovely it was, and some nurses even took pictures on their phones. That room had gone from being my personal prison cell to my sanctuary. It was where I'd been at the lowest and highest emotional points in my life, and saying goodbye to it was important. I left my pictures up for that night, as I'd have time to take it all down in the morning. I think I just watched a DVD, chilled out, and tried to take in the last two weeks.

I thought about the Grace who entered that room in a wheelchair, accompanied by my parents who I wouldn't allow to touch me. I was scared, lonely, angry and ready to give up. But that night, I was lying in that bed full of hope; feeling like the most loved, special and blessed girl in the world. I don't know how many people have had that kind of experience, but I know it can't be many.

Turning the Corner Liz

Grace's recovery was almost unbelievable. Here's how I described the first hopes at the time:

31.3.08

Hi Mel

Thanks - Grace has been very up and down, terrible mood swings and rages, but seems much better today. She says she has had an epiphany and realises that she actually was quite pretty and now looks like Gollum! She has been making lists of things she is looking forward to doing again when she is better. She has not lost any weight since Thursday so her team are very pleased with her, and crucially, she is really happy about it too.

Lots of love

Liz

Friends and family were responding to my news of the week before. My cousin expressed their concern, disbelief and helplessness.

Dear Liz

I'm so sorry to hear about Grace's troubles. It must be a terrible strain on you all. Not knowing anything much about anorexia I can't offer anything useful. It goes against all my assumptions - she's so bright and is far and away the most beautiful teenager I've ever known.

Please give her my very special love in whatever way may be appropriate

On my parents' behalf I've ordered a set of Pride & Prejudice on CDs - not the one they know and love with Irene Sutcliffe reading as I could not find that one on CD except on an American site and thought it might take ages and/or incur customs charges. I've ordered one read by Lindsay Duncan who I only know from "Rome" - she played Servilia - though apparently she's playing Lady Catherine de Burgh in a forthcoming ITV production.

Love

William

By the time I replied to this one, after Grace had started eating again, I was finding the complete turnaround perplexing and exhausting:

2.4.08

Thank you - we will look forward to Pride & Prejudice arriving. Lindsay Duncan has a lovely voice - have you not seen her in everything Stephen Poliakoff has ever written?

Yes, the last few months have been awful and who would have thought this would have ambushed Grace?? It often happens to very bright people apparently, one of the few common features between sufferers. Also good hardworking kids who don't like upsetting people. Hm.

We have been seriously worried - and she has been seeing health professionals - since New Year, and over the last few weeks she went downhill very rapidly so that hospitalisation was the only option, although all along she could be reflective and articulate about the illness and have times of being "real Grace" not "anorexic Grace" and want to get better. When she went in on Easter Tuesday she had eaten, I think, though she never ate anything in front of anyone, an orange a day for a couple of weeks. They were the only "safe" foods the anorexia would allow her to eat.

But now, with a combination of tube feeding, nurses, psychiatrists, endocrinologists, friends & relations and liquid Prozac on an empty stomach, she has suddenly started eating again - sausages, cornflakes, strawberries, salt & vinegar crisps - and realising she looks terrible and used to be quite pretty.

It is very sudden - but a false dawn is better than no light at all, and two days of her eating is better than nothing. She is definitely a bit manic - but she's eating sugar for the first time in possibly months. She is very fragile physically and mentally - she tried to run to me yesterday and fell heavily and is now quite badly bruised, and has no strength. I think it will be a long road out and I am sure the anorexic voice has not shut up for ever, but this is more than we dared hope for in the next six months, let alone this week.

Thank you for your love and thoughts - it makes a difference.

Love
Liz

To Ed, the same day:

From: Liz
Sent: 02 April 2008 14:12
To: Williams Ed
Subject: RE: Grace

Yes, me too. I feel I've been carrying round a heavy weight that isn't there any more. I talked to Martha at lunch time and she feels like us - it's amazing but we need to be careful and maybe G is a bit too excited. The psychiatrist is going to see Grace this afternoon and Martha will catch up with her afterwards to see what she thinks. There was a note on G's file to say there might be a side-effect from the Prozac. Interestingly, Martha said she'd never seen a recovery like it, but she has also never seen anyone slide so quickly into severe anorexia either. Apparently one of her colleagues in the office did see a case like this years ago. Martha says the medical staff will not rush into taking out the tube or any other action and they know that Grace is still mentally and physically very fragile. Love you, Liz

Grace was angry, upset that I was still worried. *"Why aren't you happy?"* she would say, *"Why can't you see I'm better?"*

I suppose I thought that when anorexic Grace disappeared, the old Grace would come back, but this was not the old Grace, the "real" Grace, at all. That day when she met me at the door of her room, she looked like some mythical creature, long limbs and protruding bones, her glasses and hair several sizes too big for her face, with a crazy grin on her face. She had not smiled for quite a long time and her teeth seemed huge. Her body language was entirely different: she flapped her arms and tried to run to me, looking a little like a new-born foal. She came crashing to the ground before I could reach her and bruised her ribs badly – I suppose her arms did not hold her when she fell.

Of course I was delighted that she had started eating again – but it was extreme, over the top. I had steeled myself for a long road to recovery and this was something quite different.

I didn't want to be begrudging and pessimistic, but this was not normality; it felt like a new stage of mental illness. I feared that Grace would be bipolar from now on – either depressed, withdrawn and starving herself or elated, extrovert, demanding and constantly hungry. I was worried about her coming home, that she would go downhill again, because, as she herself says, "*home is where everything went wrong*". What was it about us as a family that nurtured all those negative feelings about herself? Was there anything that we could do differently?

Coming home

Grace

The next morning after breakfast, I got all my things together from my room, and it turned out to be a bit of a job! I was leaving with a lot more than when I'd come in and I didn't have a chance of fitting all the presents, pictures, DVDs, bathing products and CDs into the weekend case I'd originally used to bring in my one change of pyjamas and the "beloved" dressing gown.

Dad requested for us to burn the thing. It had been my second skin at home and my family had grown to despise it. It was almost a physical representation of my constant ice-cold hands, always asking to turn the heating up. I was always wrapped up in that light blue fluffy dressing gown, but never cosy, never warm enough.

I took pictures of my room before I left. It looked so bleak without my bits and bobs in it; just plain and clinical.

My nurse that day was a man I'd never met before but he was very lovely and Welsh so definitely a pal. My Dad is Welsh and has taught me well to be endlessly devoted to – and proud of – my roots. I pottered about chatting to nurses and the cleaners as they did the daily jobs. I was sad to see them for the last time – they had been my family for the past two weeks and I'd barely even spoken to some of them, but they made the difference. Whether they were aware of it, consciously trying, I don't know, but I do know that every smile or *"hello"* helped me to feel like less of a waste of space and like a real, normal person.

Mum and Emily came to fetch me at 2 o'clock. I still remember what they were wearing. Even though it was April, it was chilly outside and they were both wearing jackets, jeans and boots (in Em's case her brand new Uggs). They both had their hair down - Mum's was a bit wild as usual, Emily's was wonderfully shiny and straightened.

Things were quite busy on the ward so once I'd properly checked out I didn't say any real goodbyes. I guess it's the sort of place where goodbyes are only that prominent if they're final.

We went out to the car – fresh air! Then I really did feel alive. Feeling the wind on my face was gorgeous and refreshing –and very odd. My senses had been through a complete reawakening that week, and that was the icing on the cake.

We got fish and chips on the way home. We ate them on our laps in the living room and then me and Emily made Angel Delight. It was so lovely having fun with food again.

Being at home was strange: I'd got used to the plain, sterile environment of the hospital. The presence of carpets was odd, and it felt a bit dark. I wasn't sure if I was comfortable there – it felt a bit like I was in limbo. I felt like I was a guest in a distant relative's home – I knew where everything was and how to use it, but like it would have been rude for me to use them. Mum disappeared for a nap, and Em had to go and to meet some friends, so I just watched TV downstairs. I started to feel sad then. For the first time since my big turnaround, I felt scared. Scared that I was in too deep and this big journey I was about to embark on was so vast and daunting I might not be able to do it. Was I in the right place? I was suddenly aware that home was where it had gone wrong. It was where I'd kept all those secrets and hidden my food, and felt miserable. I was so scared of feeling like that again, of being taken over by those evil voices again. I was crying and Mum came down from her nap. As soon as she saw I was crying she came and hugged me tight and I felt safe. She asked what was wrong and I told her,

"I'm just a bit scared. This is going to be really hard," I sniffed.

"Yeah, it probably will be, love. But you're strong enough to make it, you know you are."

And I did. I knew I could overcome anything. I was just worried about the unknown mystery of what my future was. I had no plan, just vague ideas and an unshakeable passion to live.

We went up to my room then, which my mum had lovingly cleaned. I lay on the bed while she unpacked my things. I wanted her to get rid of my pictures of Dan, but she wouldn't.

"I know you might not want to think about him now but one day you will treasure those memories. I'll put them somewhere safe."

I didn't understand or agree at all with her at the time, but sure enough, she was right. I do treasure that time and those memories. I only hope that when I have kids I can give such wise advice as my mum gave me. Mums have a knack of being right. They very rarely say things that make sense to teenagers – because they're wise. The sad thing is, that most of the time their words of love and wisdom don't really reach your ears until you actually want to hear them. By that time you've already learnt your lesson, and all you can take from it is the knowledge that your mum isn't a nutter. At least not completely.

Later on, once everyone had come home, we got a curry from our favourite local curry house. The Everest. I felt better once I'd had a rest and settled back in. It felt like such a treat to be in the same room as my whole family – Mum, Dad, Seth, Emily and Tilly. Just eating and watching TV with them made me feel complete. Over the next week, Mum and I just chilled out doing boring things like shopping and laundry, and watching TV. My friends came to visit me – I really appreciated their company and the effort they made to help me feel loved and special. I had appointments with Martha, and a dietician and I also met with a new psychiatrist. As there was no desperate need for regular checkups, we said I would come back in a month or so to make sure I was still progressing. It was nice to know I wasn't just written off as being "OK".

Next steps

Grace

I went to SYEDA and had a full body massage, which was gorgeous and such a treat – I felt like a princess! Definitely a world of difference to how I felt about the last one I'd had. Then I had hated being touched and "forced" to relax. I am so happy SYEDA were there before and after I was in hospital. They really offered everything I needed – all their people are understanding, compassionate and human. No questions, no weighing, just a place to be and someone to talk to.

After speaking to people at SYEDA and Martha, I'd decided to start writing about the past year. Mainly to try and make sense of it, but once I started to write, it became clear that it was my own kind of therapy. It wasn't always easy to write about the way I behaved and the things I did, but I always felt better afterwards. Confronting myself has to be the hardest thing I've done, and it continues to be.

As I started to get more and more independent, I took myself out to meet friends and I painted my bedroom as well. A few weeks after I came out of hospital I went to stay at my auntie Gill's house for a few days. I was made to feel so at home and I got really spoilt all week. My cousin kept making jokes about them adopting me. As my early birthday present, Gill took me to her hairdresser and I got my hair cut really short. I'd always wanted short hair, but never thought it would suit me – but I loved it! I felt really great about how I looked. I felt pretty and feminine and secure in that – not ashamed or big-headed. Just content. Everyone complimented me on my new look and I welcomed it. I'd always shot down anyone who complimented me (verbally, not literally) but for some reason I just didn't see the need now, and instead accepted that people wanted to be nice.

I decided I definitely didn't want to go back to school, even though all my friends were there and it made sense to just finish my A levels. I just didn't want to. I didn't see the point in doing something that made me feel like I wasn't good enough. The only reason I'd gone to sixth form was because it was the easy option. I could carry on not knowing what I wanted for another two years. But now I was thinking more clearly, I knew I loved clothes and fashion passionately – I always had. I used to draw fashion designs in the back of my Mum's notepads on holiday. And then it was clear to me that I should do what I love. Why not? It wasn't daunting or worrying, it just made sense and it was great to know what I wanted to do, not what people expected me to. I found a course at college and applied to start that September. I also found a job working in a coffee shop for the summer, which I could keep when I started college. I was really proud of myself for being so proactive and making positive changes in my life.

For my 17th birthday, mum took Emily, Tilly and me to visit my grandparents in Wales. Their house is such a special place and it felt right to be spending time with them as I recovered. My birthday was a really special day. First thing in the morning Emily and I ran down to the sea-front, and jumped into the Welsh sea from the floating pontoon – it was freezing! Then we trudged back to the house and had a cooked breakfast. My grandma had put a ring of flowers from the garden around my place at the table; it is the little gestures like that, which make them such sweet people. After breakfast I went to church with my granddad – it was just us two. When we arrived, we lit candles, and there was a list where we could write the names of people we wanted to pray for. I wrote down the names of my friends who I knew were struggling with exams. My granddad told me he had written my name in the list just a few months ago, and lit a candle of hope for me. I felt a rush of mixed emotion – deep sadness, gratitude, pride and relief that I was there, then, on my special day.

The service was small and quiet, very calm and lovely. At the end we started to get up to leave and "Amazing Grace" started to play. A long time ago when I was little, only about 3 or 4 years old, my Granddad was taking me to church and we were late. I remember trotting along by his tall frame through the graveyard outside, and as we sneaked into the back of the church the whole room was singing "Amazing Grace". We always said it was like they were welcoming me personally, even though we were late.

Today, I knew that he must have requested it specially, and I was so touched by the gesture that I started to cry. I held his hand, feeling immeasurably blessed.

After church we went back to the house for a rest, and I opened presents there, feeling especially spoilt and loved. The rest of the day, we went for afternoon tea at my uncle's new "caravan" – which was more like a chalet or flat on wheels really. We all thought it would take a lot of heaving to move it anywhere. My uncle and his girlfriend had made all sorts of lovely treats, like lavender shortbread, black cherry brownies, and tarts made with Japanese knotweed jam! I hadn't seen him in ages because we live so far away, and he's always been one of my favourite relations – so we stayed for a while catching up, talking about music and plans for the future. In the evening after dinner, me and Emily went and played on the beach and took pictures of each other jumping off rocks. That night I went to sleep feeling so happy, and proud of my family for helping me in ways they'll never know. I feel like that was the perfect way to mark my new beginning – to start my new job, college course, and who knew what else? I felt excited for my future, although it was unknown it was exciting, and an adventure I feel fully equipped for.

My 17th Birthday on the beach in Wales

Now

This is Grace's story far more than mine; and so I think it's fitting
that she should have the last word. Gradually, what I had longed
for came to pass, and Grace came through her intense recovery
period and became Grace again. She gained three stones in
weight in a month. That is not normal for anyone – but she
started eating less as she approached a healthy weight and did not
fluctuate or binge at all. She started looking well within about six
weeks, and people who saw her that summer and did not know
she had been ill suspected nothing.

I don't know if Grace would say her body is very different from
before her illness. Her face is somehow different – but she is older,
and her hair is still short, which changes your face shape. She still
gets cold hands easily, which refuse to warm up. Her periods have
only just started again, two years later.

Our relationship has changed People do change, between the
ages of 16 and 18, or even 16 and 17, so this would have happened to some extent anyway. Grace is more critical of me, more
argumentative, more independent. I think she has learnt that
it is quite possible to stay friends, or even be closer, when you
have honestly disagreed with someone. She is funny, thoughtful,
sparky, enthusiastic, loving and altogether one of my favourite
people to spend time with.

I hate to think that she felt she could not choose a career in fashion because she got messages that it was somehow not serious. When I see her working on patterns late into the night – when I know how many books she reads, the research she does, the techniques she learns – nobody can tell me this is a soft option, less demanding than English Literature. And the delight she takes in it is wonderful. She came home during her first week at college and said, *"Guess what, mum, there are TWELVE sorts of pleat!"*

I worry, of course. Hey, I'm a mother. I will always worry about something, about each of my children.

Epilogue

Grace

I don't want people to finish reading this and think,
"That's it? Two weeks in hospital and everything's perfect?"
Because it's not like that. I believe my experience was
quite miraculous, and something completely personal to
me. I still feel it was religious, but not in a way you hear
about in the mainstream. I wasn't speaking in tongues,
or possessed by the holy spirit – I was reconnecting as
well as discovering. What came from it is wholeness and
a faith. A faith in people, and their unconditional love in
dark times when some wish they were invisible. I know
I've found a spiritual way of being, but it's my own special
thing. I was changed by someone or something and I
know I'm blessed – that's enough for me and I am thankful every day.

I've just finished my first year at college, and am so happy.
The course is perfect for me. It challenges my creativity
and fuels my passion, I've been able to explore into art
and design and I've met some brilliant people. I did strug-
gle at first. The people I met are different from the people
I went to school with – and complete strangers. It made
me realise a few things about myself, and that not everyone you meet will be like-minded, or necessarily like you.

But it was exciting and interesting. I still see my friends from school and it's helped me understand myself being in a new environment.

I have had struggles in the past year – things unrelated to food. Like heartbreak, death, and complicated friendships, stress from college – but that's life. I have found that when I am feeling particularly down or stressed, the way my brain reacts is to restrict food and not let myself relax. But I recognise it as something bad, not an indulgence.

I did a self-help course at SYEDA about self-image, which I found really interesting, and it helped me get a clearer idea of how I relate to others, and myself and why. I found there were certain questions I didn't feel ready to face, about how I see my body and what I want from it. But I am asking them and answering them every day, and keeping check that I'm not veering. I have so much respect for my body now. After everything I put it through, it didn't give up. My muscles built back up, my skin healed the scars, a lot of the hair on my head fell out at first but then grew back thicker. Most importantly, my lungs keep breathing and my feet keep taking me forward. When I find myself attacking one of the parts of my body, I remember what it's been through and got me through and I say sorry.

One of the hardest things about recovery has been doing it in our current image-obsessed, self-deprecating society. When every magazine cover, TV programme or internet popup is flashing up, *"Flabby celebs"* or *"Lose 10lb in a week"* or *"New guilt-free recipes"*, it creates the idea that every woman should be trying to lose weight, trying to become the perfect being. You're seen as strange if you don't worry about your diet nowadays, and loving yourself as you are isn't always easy. When I started working at the coffee shop, a few of the women there regularly talked about diets tips and exercise and it threw me. I was almost expecting people to know not to talk about that stuff around me, because I was me. I had to check myself; remember this journey. You are repairing yourself, don't get sucked in.

Saying that, I think I'm doing a good job. I really enjoy taking care of myself, eating healthily and going to yoga with my mum. I love cooking and trying new food with different people.

My relationship with all my family is much stronger that it was before, and I know whatever happens they will always be there for me.

I can't wait to spread my wings and take on life on a bigger scale. I hope to move to Barcelona to study fashion once I've finished college, and after that, who knows?

GRACE NICHOLAS
August 2009

The last word   *Grace*

This book is me. Writing, and re-living this small yet vital
chapter of my life has been as beneficial to my health as
eating properly again. It has strengthened and calmed
and justified me in ways I never expected. From the
minute I started, I knew it would force me to revisit my
journey through anorexia, through the hardest time of
my life and help me make some sense of it. As I wrote,
it helped. I wrote things I never said, and things I wasn't
even aware that I thought. It made it easier for me to
discuss certain things with Martha or my mum, because
I'd already confronted them on my own.

I don't know what I would have done without writing; it's
how I talk to myself, because at first, everything is too
hard to say.

When I completed the first draft, I didn't want to read
it. Because it was raw. It was my truth and that made
reading it somehow harder than writing. I had to live a bit
more before I could face it again.

It's been four years since I finished the book. I am now
twenty-two; I have recently graduated from university in
London, where I studied Costume. When I went back to

edit the book, it made me realise how far away I am from that time, and how I have distanced myself mentally and physically from the person I was. I am very aware of the way it was written, and I wanted it to sound more sophisticated. But I held back, as it would be wrong to project who I am now onto this short story of how I got here.

Since completing the book and moving away from home, I have come to be very protective of the person I was then. I want to make sure that if I choose to tell someone about my experience of anorexia, that someone will value what it means. No-one truly understands unless they have experienced it first hand. Being a sufferer or a carer puts you head to head with anorexia. You can't explain what that means with words alone. I am so proud of who I am and the life I lead, and overcoming anorexia has been the building block of that.

The way I want to live changed while I was recovering, I wanted to be the best Grace I could be. I saw how the way you live and relate to people can open doors, and make a difference. And the more honest I am about myself the happier I am.

However, there are some aspects of post-anorexia that aren't so appealing. For example I still find it hard to relax, which is a mixture of wanting to achieve so much with my time but also pushing too hard. I also am terrible at doing things I don't want to do, I just don't see the point of it. If I'm talking to someone and they say, *"I don't like my job"* or *"I hate doing this"*, I just say *"Stop it then! Stop wasting your time!"* I know that is annoying for some people but I believe it. If something makes you miserable, and it's not a means to an end, don't waste your energy.

Recovery takes a long time and old habits are hard to break. Like the habit I have of putting myself down, which I've had since I discovered it can make people laugh (roughly aged 5). I'm still learning how to accept a compliment. I've gone through battles since then and will continue to. And I do have demons; there is still a small bird there that is scared of gaining weight. I'm ashamed of it, because it's ugly. It's a bird I don't like. When I chose to recover, I promised myself there would be no going back and the ugly bird feels regressive. But the older I get the easier it is to ignore. I know the patterns of it now too. If I'm feeling depressed it will be there, also if I'm feeling under pressure from work or a relationship. I can understand why I hear it and more importantly why I shouldn't listen to it.

We were just living our lives and along came this illness that tried to tear us apart from ourselves. But we kept going, and when I wasn't fighting, my family and friends fought for me. They fought for me with their love and devotion and didn't let anorexia take me away. Through their texts, emails, hot water bottles and oranges, they gave me the courage to stare my illness in the face and tell it I was better than anorexia. I'm worth more than the mess it created.

I do think that we take it in turns to fight for one another, that is just how it will go sometimes. I thrive on being able to fight for my loved ones now, to use the strength they gave me. Everyone mentioned in the book, and others too, showed me what it means to care and love someone back to life, which I will never forget.

February 2014